Advance Praise

You've heard me say, "The point of a book should be to change your behavior in a meaningful way." That is exactly what Peggy's book does. She provides the ideas, research, and real-life examples. She takes this a step further by providing you with specific actionable steps for you to take and improve your life immediately. –Hal Elrod, international keynote speaker and best-selling author of *The Miracle Morning and The Miracle Equation*

Dr. Peggy DeLong's book is chock full of useful ideas immediately accessible to anyone interested in adding happiness to their life. Peggy's stories make it relatable, interesting, and fun—and it's all backed by research. In short, it's a roadmap to joy. –Jenny Meyer Colman, MD, Psychiatrist, Bard and Marist Colleges

In a heartfelt, authentic way, Peggy brings conventional wisdom to life. She intertwines deeply personal life stories with science to validate her recommendations for ways to take control of your own joy. You will feel empowered and optimistic when you let Peggy's words, delivered with kindness and compassion, wash over you. –Julie Kahn, Associate Partner & Executive Recruiter, JUEL Consulting

Dr. DeLong's empathic heart, crystalline memories, keen intellect, sincere gratitude, and creative ingenuity all burst forth from this profoundly engaging and helpful book. *Feeling Good* has something for everyone, especially parents who could open this book up to any page for insights to immediately improve their own family experiences. –Kristen Henderson, MFA, MSW, poet and author of *Drum Machine and Of My Maiden Smoking*

In *Feeling Good*, Dr. Peggy Doherty DeLong makes recommendations backed up by scientific research, telling life stories that motivate readers to take action. I don't know anyone who wouldn't benefit from reading this book when they're feeling overwhelmed, and then reading it again when they're not. It's an entertaining and inspiring guide to help each of us rewire our brains for joy. **–Lyle Smith, Founder, Nymblesmith and Creator/Host of The Story Forge Podcast**

Expect a feeling of deep satisfaction after reading Dr. Peggy DeLong's new book, *Feeling Good*. It addresses universal emotional challenges with a personal voice that makes you feel like she's sitting with you at your kitchen table. This gem of a book offers "Take Action" accessible guides at the end of each well-crafted chapter, all in the name of finding happiness. **–Julie Maloney, award-winning author and founder/director of *Women Reading Aloud*, an international writing organization**

In her new book, Dr. Peggy Delong reminds us of this essential truth: "You are a powerful human being." During the most challenging times, her wisdom is especially important. With science-backed tips from her own childhood and practice, Dr. Peggy empowers you to live your best life with joy! **–Sha Nacino, Keynote Speaker on Gratitude & Creativity, Founder, World Gratitude Summit™**

Step-by-step, Dr. Peggy Doherty DeLong walks her readers through ways to cultivate happiness. She explains everything from exercising during the pandemic to the power of forgiveness. The suggestions in-between are practical, soulful, and life-affirming. This is a simple, yet profound book about fostering happiness. **–Megan McDowell, MSW, LPC, Founder/ Visionary of Heartworks Foundation**

"Life isn't fair." What a way to start a book! At a time when it's become cool to complain or "win the internet" with sarcasm and snark, Dr. Peggy's book brings readers back to a fundamental truth: Life happens, and you can be happy as it does. Her message is a joyful call for responsibility and transformation that will make you smile and that keeps delivering with practical steps the world needs right now. –Sarah Walton, Business Mentor, Author & Speaker, the voice behind the Game On Girlfriend Podcast

Dr. Peggy DeLong's newest book illuminates a comprehensive guide for joyful practice, movement, connection, and mindfulness in everyday life. As a mother, friend, nature photographer, and animal rescuer, I can attest that *Feeling Good* is a gift to anyone searching for practical, easy steps to support and ignite happiness awareness and activity. –Kristen Escalante, Former CEO Heartworks OC and owner of Mindfully Focused Photography

Dr. DeLong personifies someone who exudes joy, happiness, and a sense of mental well-being. It's easy to assume her special glow is the result of being lucky or having a privileged life. However, Dr. DeLong has met her fair share of challenges and losses. In her latest book, *Feeling Good*, she lets us in on her secrets to living a happy life. By sharing her personal stories along with the latest scientific research, Dr. DeLong lays out the special tools we need to create the life we all long for—one filled with purpose, happiness, and fulfillment. –Dr. Robi Ludwig, TV personality, Author, and Psychotherapist

Dr. Peggy DeLong's new book came along at just the right time! In these challenging times, Dr. Peggy's wisdom, humor, and guidance was my saving grace on many days. The inspirational quotes and action items will lead you to happiness and help you find joy in life, no matter your challenges. Brava! –Susan Striano, LCSW, Adjunct Professor and Social Work Manager

Dr. Peggy DeLong has done it again! In her third book, *Feeling Good*, Dr. Peggy shares heartfelt family experiences—along with years of clinical and research-based practices—all within one real-world, take-control book. She provides valuable, research-based techniques that will allow you to begin your journey of genuine joy, contentment, and gratitude. You'll feel empowered, resilient, and yes, happy. **–Reesa Weingold, PhD, LPC, Certified School Psychologist**

In *Feeling Good*, Dr. Peggy DeLong truly meets you wherever you are, empowering individuals from any background or circumstance to live a more joyful life. She elevates concepts of creating more happiness by guiding readers to apply her suggestions in their own lives and easily take action. Reading Dr. DeLong's book feels like the sigh of relief that comes after chatting with a wise, supportive friend. **–Kelly McFadden, Mindset Coach**

After my fourteenth appointment of the week as a Career and Life Coach, I felt completely drained and did something coaches should never do—I got short with my client! I immediately apologized, but he said he barely noticed my curtness. After the appointment, I started berating myself. Then I opened *Feeling Good* to a random page and landed on Chapter 6—Listen to Music! Singing and dancing to Pharrell's song, "Happy" for five minutes got me back to helping clients and being present for them no matter what. Thank you Dr. DeLong for creating this handy tool to keep my spirits high and my purpose alive and well.**–Amy Ames, CPCC, Career and Life Coach**

FEELING

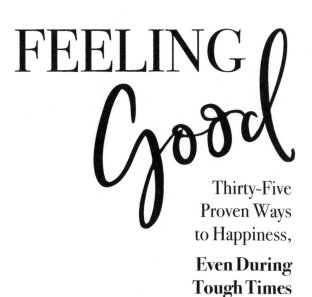

Good

Thirty-Five
Proven Ways
to Happiness,

**Even During
Tough Times**

Dr. Peggy Doherty DeLong

FEELING Good

Thirty-Five Proven Ways to Happiness, Even During Tough Times

Dr. Peggy Doherty DeLong

PEACOCK PROUD
P · R · E · S · S
Phoenix, Arizona

Editors:
    Laura L. Bush, PhD, PeacockProud.com
    Wendy Ledger, VoType.com
Cover and Interior Layout:
    Jana Galvan
Portrait Photographer:
    Carley Storm of Carley Storm Brand Co., carleystorm.com

TABLE OF
Contents

*I dedicate this book to my family of origin,
including my late father, Bill Doherty; my mother, Carol Doherty;
my sister, Debbie Nazario; and my brothers, Brian and David Doherty.
Thank you for your role in creating our home environment, filled
with love, laughter, and so much joy. It was in the comfort of your
love and security that these methods were originally
discovered and enjoyed.*

*To the family I have created with my husband, John,
including our daughters, Carly and Morgan, and our son, Jamie.
May you all always know that the power lies within you to create your
happiness and a life filled with joy, even on your difficult days.
Especially on your difficult days.*

Introduction

All my life, people have said to me, "You're so happy!" followed by the question, "What do you do to be so happy?" Some have even asked me this question with skepticism or disdain. When I would give an example or two of things I do, they'd often say, "Well, that's easy for YOU. You're a happy person!"

But the truth is, I'm like everybody else. I've just been blessed to have stumbled upon some things that worked for me, so I stuck with them! I began learning coping methods when I was a young girl and couldn't articulate the feelings of sadness or anxiety, which I described to my mother as "that funny feeling in my tummy." I learned how to make "that funny feeling in my tummy" go away: I drew. I read. I had a friend over for a play date. I made latch hook rugs.

It also probably helped that I was raised by a child psychiatrist. But I must say that my father never directly taught me coping skills. They were more a way of life in my household. For example, my family already built time into my schedule for exercising and getting outdoors. My father never said, "Go outside and get some exercise. It will be good for your mental health." Instead, we simply skied and biked together. He never said, "Talk about your feelings. It will help." Instead, my parents fostered a safe environment where they welcomed and encouraged conversation, and where we were free to express our emotions. We regularly had family dinners, and my father was a big fan of board games, which is when our discussions took place. Sometimes we would reflect on the day's enjoyable activities. Other times, we talked about our feelings and resolving conflict. My parents were always accepting and non-judgmental. My mother's lap was also a great place to privately share my emotions or simply to cry when the words did not come easily.

In 1994, my fiancé and my father died within six weeks of each other. In the days and weeks after their deaths, I seldom felt joy. When I did feel happy, it felt like a foreign experience. However, I never felt like I was going to "fall apart." In my first book, *I Can See Clearly Now: A Memoir about Love, Grief, and Gratitude*, I talked about how I was able to rebuild my life after such loss. As time passed, I was able to live my life with more joy than ever before. People would tell me, "I'm so glad you're OK. In fact, you're more than OK. You're happy. Many people don't recover after what you've been through." They would wonder how I did it.

I was asked these questions many times, in many ways. At first, I wondered, "What in the world do I do to give people this impression?" I began to think long and hard about what I do to "be so happy." Later, as a mental health professional, I realized if I could share my insights and experiences on what I do to be happy, I could provide a valuable service for others in the world.

Ultimately, I came up with thirty-five different things I do to be happy. Now these are not things I do every day, but they're simple enough to practice often, especially on your very worst days. Of course, you can do these things on your great days, too, but I truly love the idea of having things to do on bad days—when you need them the most. In fact, I was editing this book in the midst of COVID-19, and I really put these strategies to the test. I'm happy to report that they are now "pandemic-tested."

Some of these practices revolve around mindset. Some are solo activities. In some, you interact with others. Some don't take much time at all, and some can last a few hours. Some involve planning, and some can be totally spontaneous.

I also want to stress that my goal is not for me—or you—to maintain a high level of happiness all the time. That simply isn't natural. Besides, trying to maintain high levels of happiness would be quite exhausting— not to mention disappointing! When achieved, happiness is wonderful. However, it can be short-lived, and it feels elusive when you're going through difficult times. On the other hand, you can always experience joy. Even on a horrible day, during a difficult situation, in the middle of a worldwide pandemic, it *is* possible to experience joy.

In this book, I have given each of my practices its own chapter. Each chapter begins with an inspirational quote, setting the stage for the power of that concept. Within the chapter, I have demonstrated how this idea can cultivate joy in your life through personal examples from my own life and others. In addition, I have provided research to support the effectiveness of these ideas. As a psychologist, I know the importance of backing up what I say with scientific research. I don't want to waste your time. I want to provide you with ideas that have been clinically studied and proven to give you effective access to joy and fulfillment in your life.

Each chapter ends with the most important component—action steps for you to take. These simple steps can help you start to cultivate joy in your life. I have designed these steps so that you can do them even if you're low on time, energy, or money. By completing these steps, you will be on your way to living in your own happiness.

Consider looking at your happiness as your "job" to do. In my life, I've learned that happiness is not a one-and-done deal where you do some simple things and then you're good to go. No. Happiness doesn't work that way. It takes practice, just like everything else. All practice is simply (1) focused attention and (2) repetition. Those two things are all it takes to "practice joy." Focus your attention on finding joy and repeat. Every day.

Here's the great news. If you do these steps, you will feel good. I'm not going to ask you to do things that feel awful and tell you that you need to punish yourself on the way to happiness. No. You will feel good while you're on your way to finding your joy.

My goal for you in reading this book is that you see some ideas that you already do, but now you can practice them with increased intention and purpose, knowing that the science shows that action is beneficial for your mental health. I also hope to introduce you to some new ideas that you can incorporate into your life and begin to feel, see, and experience joy in a way you never have before.

As you begin this book, it's important for you to believe that you have the power to control your thoughts and actions and increase the joy in your life. The more you believe in your power for self-healing and happiness, the more likely you will take action and use these ideas. Now let's get started.

Chapter 1

Accept That "Life Is Not Fair"

*"The happiest people don't worry too much about
whether life is fair or not. They just get on with it."*
–Andrew Matthews, *Happiness in Hard Times*

When bad things happen to us, we will be happier when we accept that life is not fair. We can take a moment to feel sorry for ourselves and feel all the emotions that come with that attitude. But then we need to decide what we are going to do about it rather than continue to ruminate about the injustice of this situation.

Research supports the benefits of letting go of this negativity. One study, "Counted Blessings Versus Burdens" by Emmons and McCullough, found that people who wrote about what they were grateful for reported significantly higher levels of well-being compared to a group that wrote negatively about experiences.[1] The implication is that our mental health improves when we are able to move past what is not fair or not going well in our lives.

I first learned this concept when I was a child. Over and over again, my father told me that life was not fair. He said it in the most loving way. I did not feel that I had to "be tough" or "just get over it." If I complained about a situation, my father would say, "What are you going to do about it?" He didn't come right out and say that I had control over how I responded, but that was the message that he let me figure out. When something felt unfair, my father continually encouraged me to think of solutions and take action. Through his words, I rose to the challenge and enjoyed the outcomes.

My father not only taught me this lesson, he lived it himself. He grew up as an only child in Union City, New Jersey, in a tiny, two-bedroom apartment. As a young child, I visited this home a few times when my grandmother still lived there. Many locks adorned the front door, and we walked down a very dark hallway to the staircase to the second floor. The apartment was at the top of the dark staircase. Once inside, the apartment was much brighter, but it was not welcoming. My grandmother covered all of the furniture in thick plastic. As a child wearing shorts, I was uncomfortable sitting anywhere. It was a far cry from the soft furniture in my home.

My grandfather captained a tugboat on the Hudson River, and my grandmother worked in a lightbulb factory. They had very little money, but there were lightbulbs everywhere. They had difficulty putting food on the table. Even with two working parents, times were tough, requiring them to make some difficult economic decisions.

To help pay their bills, my father's parents took in a tenant. The tenant rented my father's bedroom, and my father then only had a closet for his room. As a young boy, my father did not understand why this had to happen. But he made the best of the situation and turned his closet "bedroom" into a fort with just enough room for a small mattress on the floor. "I lined up all my toys along the side," he said. "Then I put a small lamp in the corner for light and hung my clothes on hangers on the bar above me. I used to run my foot along the bottoms of the clothes and make them move!"

Having a closet for a bedroom doesn't seem desirable or fair for any child. However, when my father told this story, I never heard "life is not fair" in his voice. Instead, he transformed his experience of having a closet for a bedroom into an adventure.

I believe this experience inspired my father to seek out open space in his adulthood after earning his medical degree. But first let me explain how he overcame "unfairness" and earned that degree. He was determined not to live a life of poverty. He worked hard during high school, earning an acceptance to Georgetown University. He then pushed himself even further in college to earn acceptance into Georgetown's medical school. He often told stories of how his classmates came from old family money and boarding schools. They didn't need to have jobs while in school. My father, on the other hand, always had a job. Rather than complain or talk about how this was unfair, when he told stories to my siblings and me, he always told them with a sense of pride and humor. I particularly loved hearing his story of how he took on one last shift as a waiter in order to have enough money to replace his car's flat tire, so he could get home from Washington, D.C. to New Jersey after graduating from medical school for his first job at St. Michael's Hospital in Newark. He was very happy to make it for his first day of work because it was on that day that he met my mother.

After working for a few years as a psychiatrist, he sought property away from the city. He was so proud to purchase a home surrounded by trees and grass. As if that wasn't enough, he bought a trailer at a family campground in the Pocono Mountains of Pennsylvania, where we spent every waking moment outside in nature during summer weekends. The little boy who grew up with a closet for a bedroom became a man who had immense gratitude for open space.

When I was fourteen years old, I had an opportunity to figure out what I was going to do with a situation that felt unfair. At the time, I was the youngest employee working at a day-care center in the infant room.

When it came time to do the dirty jobs, they usually called my name. "Peggy, go change Johnny's diaper. It stinks." It didn't seem fair that I was always the one who had to clean up baby vomit or change poopy diapers. After all, we all had the same written job responsibilities and were all paid minimum wage. The only difference was my age. I gathered up the courage and announced, "Just because I'm the youngest doesn't mean I should be given all the yucky jobs." Rather than wallow in how unfair this was and not do anything about it, I remembered my father's question, "What are you going to do about it?" Then I spoke up for myself by talking to the Director. The result was even division among all workers to complete these unpleasant tasks.

I will never forget the response of one of my coworkers, a grandmother in her sixties. She said that never in her life was she able to stand up for herself like I did. "I was even more impressed because you are only fourteen," she told me. "You taught me that it can be done, and that I should speak up for myself as well." She didn't need to work, but she enjoyed children. The job gave her something to do since her children were grown, and her grandchildren lived far away.

At first this made me sad for her. But then I decided to focus on the beautiful outcome: she was going to speak up for herself. This happened thirty-eight years ago, but I still remember her name and how she always looked as though she had just come out of a salon with her coiffed hair. She was always dressed in pressed slacks and a feminine blouse as if she were going out to lunch with her girlfriends, not going to get spit up on after burping an infant. She wore lovely perfume that reminded me of my grandmother.

Throughout my life, I also learned that life is all about perception. If we look at a situation one way, then yes, it's not fair, and we may feel discouraged, sad, or beaten down. But if we look at it another way, we may realize we don't really have it so bad after all. Back in 1994, this idea about the power of perception really hit home. My fiancé, Scott, had been diagnosed with a very aggressive form of cancer just three months into our engagement. I thought that it was incredibly unfair that this time of my life that I had looked forward to since being a little girl was now tainted with sadness, fear, and uncertainty.

During his first hospital stay, Scott's roommate, Kevin, also happened to be in his twenties and engaged to be married. Kevin suggested that I read a few books, including *Love, Medicine, and Miracles* by Bernie Siegel, M.D. I devoured that best seller. I hung on to every word of hope the book conveyed. Then I learned that Bernie Siegel was coming to a speaking engagement in New Jersey, right near me. I just had to go.

The large conference room at a hotel was so packed that people were standing up lining the walls. One of the first things Dr. Siegel did was ask the audience members to raise their hands if they thought that life was unfair. Almost every hand went up. Then he said, "Since all of you raising your hands think that life is unfair, then it really must be fair." He pointed out that since we all had something to complain about—something not going "right" in our lives—then life did not discriminate. In other words, life is "unfair" for all of us, so life must really be fair!

Even though I grew up learning to take action when I thought that life was unfair, as soon as I experienced the biggest tragedy of my life to that point, I still had difficulty coping with it. How could life treat me so wrong with my fiancé dying from cancer? How could it possibly become even more unjust with my father dying suddenly six weeks later? The looks of sympathy people gave me only reaffirmed how unfair life was to me—what a raw deal I had been given.

Despite having a history of doing something positive when I thought that life was unfair, I struggled a lot when I lost my fiancé and my father at almost the same time. Then I remembered that Bernie Siegel said we all struggle. I also sought out books to read about other people's pain, some worse than mine, to help drive the idea into my head that no one goes through life without suffering. One book that helped me tremendously was Viktor Frankl's *Man's Search for Meaning.* Dr. Frankl endured years of horrifying terror in the Nazi concentration camps. Out of his suffering, he developed an approach to psychotherapy that he called logotherapy. The basic premise is that our fundamental human drive is our search for meaning in our lives. Like me, Dr. Frankl lost more than one family member in a short period of time. Unlike me, he suffered unspeakable circumstances in concentration camps. While I could not possibly comprehend that horror, I could relate to the loss of family members. He lost his wife, father, mother, and brother, yet he was still able to find meaning in life through love for his fellow human being, purposeful work, and courage when faced with adversity. Frankl also highlighted that even when we have everything and everyone taken from us, we still have the power and freedom to choose our attitude.

Through reading Viktor Frankl's account, I recalled the prompting that my father taught me: "What are you going to do about it?" Dr. Frankl then urged, "How are you going to find meaning in your life?" Finding meaning and purpose in my life required me to move beyond thinking that life was unfair.

Take Action

1. Catch yourself thinking, "This isn't fair." Acknowledge it. It's important not to stuff it down right away because what we don't acknowledge and address finds a way to rear its ugly head. Trust me, it will. So recognize it and have a little pity party. Then follow the next steps, so you don't get stuck there.

2. Make a list of two things that you can do right away about something in your life that's unfair. Then list at least one thing you can do that may take more time. Sometimes, just writing these things down can

make us feel better. But don't stop there. Make a point to do these things!

3. If you find that you cannot do anything about the unfairness, you can change how you think about it. On a piece of blank paper, draw a line down the middle. On the left-hand side, write a thought or feeling about why it's not fair. Then on the right-hand side, challenge yourself to come up with a more useful thought or feeling. Once the right-hand side is finished, write those ideas on a 3x5 index card and then review it every day. This way, you are retraining your brain to think about your situation differently. So even though you may not have thought you could do something about it, you just did! You changed the way you thought about it, and that is monumental.

Nature and the Arts

Chapter 2

Get Outside in Nature

"Climb the mountains and get their good tidings.
Nature's peace will flow into you as sunshine flows into the trees."
–John Muir

Find some time every day to get outside, even it if it just for five minutes, and especially if you are stuck in an office all day. It's really hard to stay angry or frustrated when you are outside in natural beauty. Scientists have discovered that people report an overall better sense of well-being after being in nature. One study found that group walks in nature were associated with decreased depression, stress, and low mood, and increased positive mood and overall mental health.[2] It's not just the exercise. People tend to have improved mental health when they have access to open space.[3] Another study found that compared to indoor exercise, people who engaged in physical activity in nature reported less anger, tension, confusion and depression, and increased energy.[4]

Nature has healing, therapeutic, and creative powers. It's why people escape to the mountains, to the country, or to the beach when they need some peace. It's why writers and artists go to beautiful settings to work on their craft. It's why people go on retreats in nature to replenish their souls. It's why people to turn the beauty of nature for emotional and physical healing. Simply put, nature heals.

One study demonstrated the positive impact of walking in nature.[5] The study compared those who walked ninety minutes in a park-like setting with those who had walked along a busy highway. They examined "brooding" or "morbid rumination." This is when we cannot stop thinking about the negative, what is wrong within ourselves, or how things are going wrong in our lives. This is important to address because our thoughts are related to our feelings, and brooding can lead to depression and anxiety.[6] The study found that those who had walked in nature had less brooding. They were not as consumed by negativity as they had been before. It wasn't the walking that led to the decrease in negativity, as the group that walked by the highway did not experience the same decrease in negativity. The important factor was being in nature. This study suggests that the mental health benefits of walking can be maximized by walking in nature.

In another study, college students took pictures of items in nature or human-made items and noted how the items made them feel. Those who took pictures of items in nature felt more connected to nature, other people, and life.[7]

Another group of researchers examined what exactly it is about nature that is so healing. Study participants were assigned to one of three groups. One group looked at a video of awe-inspiring scenery. Another group looked at a video of funny animals. Another group looked at neutral landscape. All three groups were instructed to passively watch and then to pay attention to changes in perspectives. In their study of the groups that had watched funny animals and neutral landscapes, researchers discovered that their functional MRIs showed increased activity in the default mode network, a brain system that encouraged their minds to wander or focus on themselves. On the other hand, the researchers learned that the group that looked at awe-inspiring nature did not demonstrate a difference in the default mode network. This suggests awe stops us from ruminating about our problems and stressors, leading to increased happiness.[8]

Think about it. It makes so much sense! When was the last time you witnessed a beautiful sunrise or sunset, lovely flower, or wildlife creature in nature? Were you thinking about your troubles of the day at the same time you enjoyed your view? Probably not. Awe stops negative thinking in its tracks.

If you really want to maximize the benefits of being in nature, seek out trees and water. In his book, *Forest Bathing: How Trees Can Help You Find Health and Happiness*, Qing Li states that being in a forest improves sleep, lowers blood pressure, decreases anxiety, and decreases physiological stress. He encourages us all to practice this "forest bathing."[9] Regarding water, Wallace Nichols writes in his book, *Blue Mind: The Surprising Science That Shows How Being Near, In, On, or Under Water Can Make You Happier, Healthier, More Connected, and Better at What You Do*, that we have a biological connection to water, and that being around various forms of water triggers an immediate response in our brains. Neurochemicals that induce relaxation and foster wellness are released in the brain when we hear and see water.[10]

Unfortunately, people are spending less and less time outdoors. Instead of meeting up with friends to bike around the neighborhood, kids are "meeting up" inside, online. It saddens me that they do not even realize what they are missing. Studies show that spending time outdoors is associated with decreased levels of anxiety and depression.[11] The great thing is, there is an easy fix. Get outside. Yes, I know it sounds simplistic. That's because it is!

I am blessed that my parents introduced me to the healing power of nature when I was a very young girl. Both of my parents grew up in cities, my mother in East Orange, NJ, and my father in Union City, NJ. They spent their childhoods in cities and did not spend much time outside of city life. This experience inspired them to seek out the outdoors in their adulthood. When my father earned enough money to purchase a home, he chose a town with bucolic countryside. Back in 1971, when my parents first purchased our home, Bernardsville was full of rural dirt roads, large farms, and horses and cows. Jeriann was my next-door neighbor and best friend. In fact, she still is! We often walked out her driveway and crossed Lloyd Road near the corner of Mendham Road to feed the cows some grass, right from our three-year-old little hands. As we walked toward the wooden, split rail fence, the wild, prickly grass scratched against the young, soft skin around our ankles and calves. The cows eagerly approached us from the other side of the fence, taking the green offering that we just picked from around our feet, and leaving behind a wet, slimy tangible thank you on our hands as we giggled with delight.

As if that was not enough nature, my father wanted his children to have even more wilderness and open space. So he purchased a large trailer with two tip-outs that we kept on a small rented plot of land full of lush, green ferns and thick rhododendron at Trails End in Shahola Falls, Pennsylvania. There, we spent every minute outside. There, my love for the outdoors blossomed.

I climbed the trees on our property, hoping that one of the thousands of gypsy moth caterpillars did not fall on my face. My father took us fishing, where I experienced the prickly sensation of the fiberglass of the boat under my skin and the stinky smell of the fish we caught. But most of all, I remember the emotions of being in nature. Joy. Happiness. Peace.

During my wonderful childhood, we spent every summer weekend at the trailer, exploring the woods, biking, swimming, and looking for salamanders. In the winter, we spent every weekend skiing. This set the foundation for my appreciation for the healing power of the outdoors, particularly the mountains. When I became old enough to choose how to handle anxiety, depression, and sad and stressful situations, I always turned to being outside in nature.

Throughout all of my years of school, I was an overachiever and put unnecessary stress on myself. I would counteract the effects of that stress with hikes and walks in nature. This energized me, and the stress and anxiety felt less heavy. I was blessed to have many places in nature to visit. The Primrose Trail at Jockey Hollow was one of my favorite places while I was a senior in high school. I loved that it was a narrow, single track trail with many wooden planks over small brooks and the soothing sounds of rippling water. I could hear the song of my favorite bird, the wood thrush, deep in those woods. I also found that on a clear day, I could stand in natural beauty and see New York's Twin Towers in the distance from the one clearing at a high point of the trail.

Often, when we are exercising, we don't feel the benefit, the reward, until the workout is over. However, being in nature, the effects are immediate. As soon as I got out of my car and walked to the trailhead, I experienced the healing power of the deep woods, streams, and giant skunk cabbage.

When college studying became too overwhelming, I took half-day breaks and headed to Sugarbush Mountain to ski. Fortunately, Sugarbush had a deal where college students could buy a season pass for a discount, only $200. Many people did not understand why I would go by myself. While I love skiing with others, there are times that I simply need to be alone. When I am by myself, I am not distracted by conversation and can fully take in my surroundings. I can be more present and connect with nature. Yes, skiing is thrilling and a stress-reliever in itself. But it was the mountains that provided me with serenity and relaxation.

As I skied during the week, there were never many people out skiing. So I was alone on my chairlift rides. I would get to the top, decide which way I was going to ski down, and then choose a midway spot to stop, sit on a rock, and just breathe in the cool mountain air. My half-days in solitude on the mountain were in stark contrast to my existence on campus. Busy. Stressed. Loud. Social. Academic. I don't know what other students did to cope with the stress. But I knew for sure that being in the mountains was my salve.

I am grateful for the predictable soothing and healing powers of nature. Knowing that I could count on nature to be there for me after my fiancé died was a true blessing. While I very much needed human comfort, human compassion, human company, and human conversation, the mountains literally and figuratively saved me from my intense grief.

It is not surprising then that after my fiancé died, my father told me that when his time came, he wanted to die on a chairlift. After my fiancé's death, my father and I had many conversations about death in an attempt to make sense of our profound loss. My father said that when it was his time to leave the physical world, he wanted to die on a chairlift because that is where he felt closest to God, breathing in the cool mountain air. Two weeks later, he died on a chairlift. He had a sudden heart attack on a chairlift ride at Okemo Mountain on an early season ski trip to Vermont. While way too young, he died exactly the way he wanted to, and it simply does not get any better or more beautiful than that. The young boy who grew up with a closet for a bedroom died in the vast openness of the mountains.

I then turned to nature and the mountains with a sense of urgency, an even stronger need to heal. But first to grieve. So nature and the mountains took on a new role. Before I could allow the healing power to begin, I first used nature to contain my grief. A stream, the deep woods, a meadow, the mountains—it didn't matter what it was. Being in nature was simply part of my grieving process. In nature, I could cry while walking, or sit on a rock and weep. My grief didn't offend or scare nature. It wasn't too much for nature to bear. Nature was strong enough to contain all of my sorrow. Nature became my healer.

Take Action

1. Think about what types of landscape bring you the most peace. The ocean, the woods, the mountains, a lake, a stream? Then make a point to visit these places. Follow the research and seek out trees and water.

If it's not possible to do during the day, make a plan for when you can schedule some time. Do this regularly, and make it predictable. Make it known to your heart that it will come, on the days that you cannot be there.

2. Even if you only have five minutes, don't underestimate the power of nature. Find ways to incorporate that five minutes of being in nature into your daily schedule. If you're in a city and taking a bus or subway home, get off at a different spot near a park, or take a moment to stand next to and touch a tree. Or go ahead and hug that tree! If you are blessed to live in an area surrounded by beautiful nature, don't take it for granted, even on your busiest of days. While running errands, stop for five minutes to get out of your car, take some deep breaths, and take in the beauty around you.

3. On the days when you simply are unable to spend time in nature, visualize. Visualize one of your favorite scenes in nature. What does it look like? What do you smell? What can you hear or touch? Recall it in as much vivid detail as possible. Did you know that our brains cannot tell the difference between living an event and remembering an event? This helps us harness the healing power of nature simply through visualization.

4. Keep a picture of your favorite peaceful scene in nature at work or on your nightstand. Looking at photographs of nature has similar mental health and physiological benefits to actually being there.

5. If you'd like additional inspiration and resources regarding connecting with nature, you'll find it in my monthly membership, Feeling Good with Dr. Peggy, archived in the month of March 2020.

Chapter 3

Exercise

"A vigorous five-mile walk will do more good
for an unhappy but otherwise healthy adult than
all the medicine and psychology in the world."
–Paul Dudley White

Physical exercise is a very effective way of elevating mood. By physical exercise, I am referring to anything that moves your body – walking, running, Pilates, strength training, yoga, playing sports, and more. There are countless studies that demonstrate the mental health benefits of exercise.[12] In fact, doctors are now prescribing physical exercise to treat depression. Physical activity increases serotonin in the brain, which helps to elevate mood and limit the effects of stress. Exercise produces endorphins, the "feel good" chemicals in the brain, which help to reduce physical and emotional pain. Exercise also causes heart rate to speed up, which increases norepinephrine, which helps us to cope with stress more effectively.[13]

One study found that exercise boosts mood right afterwards and also had long-term benefits. Physical activity was as effective as medication for treating depression. In a follow-up study, those who had continued to exercise regularly had less symptoms of depression. The researchers concluded that exercise not only helped with alleviating symptoms of depression, but also helped to prevent relapse.[14]

Studies demonstrate that exercise also helps with anxiety. Smits and Otto found that sixty volunteers with a heightened sensitivity to anxiety demonstrated significant improvements after participating in a two-week exercise program as compared to the group that had not participated in the program.[15]

Physical exercise, whether that is an intense cardio workout biking ten miles, or yoga poses while remaining on one 24" x 68" yoga mat, diminishes the intensity of unwanted, uncomfortable, or painful emotions. Moving the body and discharging physical energy decreases the intensity of anger, assuages grief and sorrow, and softens sadness and disappointment.

During COVID-19, many people turned to exercise to help them cope with the stress, anxiety, and fear. In the beginning, there were many different ways to exercise, including using national, state, and county parks. As the virus spread and options were limited, people became quite resourceful in seeking exercise. My friends Kathryn and Andrea, who are yoga instructors, conducted their classes online. Others used the stairs inside their houses or apartment buildings. People like me who are typically inclined to choose cardiovascular activities had the opportunity and time to try something new, or something long-neglected, such as simple stretching!

Keep these ideas in mind when using exercise to help with your mood:

- Do something you enjoy. If you don't know what that is, try new things to discover it. If you don't enjoy it, you are less likely to stick with it.
- Do not take on too much at once. If your goal is to run three miles, and you have never run that distance, start with one mile. You risk injury if you take on too much at once. In addition, try not to put too much pressure on yourself to go farther or faster. The goal is for it to be enjoyable.
- Find a partner or a group through Facebook, Meet Up, etc.

- Use technology to monitor your progress, provide feedback, and make it more fun. Some apps to try are Strava, My Fitness Pal, Nike+ Running Club, Map My Run, and Map My Ride.
- Put it on your calendar and consider it as important as an appointment with someone else.
- Have an accountability partner. This could be someone you exercise with or someone you check in with every day.
- Make sure you have your doctor's "okay."

Exercising with others has the added benefit of increasing social connection, and research shows that connecting with others helps with resilience and happiness.[16] In other words, having a strong social support network is an important factor in resilience at any age. Exercise or a sport can help maintain lifelong relationships. At fifty-two years old, I am still friends with many people I used to ski with as a young teenager. My group of crazy mountain bikers and skiers led to meeting my husband, so I am particularly grateful for these activities.

Looking back on my own life, exercise has played a crucial role in alleviating stress and improving my mood. It has become my "go-to" thing when I need a quick mood boost. For six years, I coordinated a weekly walk for women. I decided to form the group after reading an article about the mental health benefits of not just walking, not just nature, and not just being with others, but the special outcome when these three ingredients are mixed together – the benefits of walking with others in nature.17

I simply started with an announcement in various local Facebook groups about my intention to start this group. It was supposed to be just for the winter, to help people get outside when they are inclined to stay indoors. On the day of the first walk, it was 20 degrees outside and windy. One person showed up! But that was just enough for me to keep the group going. The group grew quickly, and members asked that I continue to organize the walks after the winter. So it became a group that walked throughout the entire year for six years.

After each walk, I noticed the smiles, laughter, hugs, and exchange of contact information among the women. I am grateful for the opportunity to see with my own eyes how walking with others in nature has a positive impact on overall well-being. The fact that the women kept coming back also demonstrated to me that they benefited from the experience. One woman in particular has a special place in my heart. She came to almost every walk. She supported other women with her words of wisdom, life experiences, and encouragement. She is an active grandmother of eleven grandchildren under the age of ten, and she lives a life of adventure. She is an inspiration to me, and I know that other group members feel the same way. I never would have met her without this group.

People are busy, and they simply do not have the time or interest to engage in activities that they do not find worthwhile. Their return to this group was a message to me that they valued the experience. The smiles and laughter at the end of the walks told me that their moods had been enhanced through this experience.

Take Action

1. Do what you enjoy. If you don't know what that is yet, try some things out.

2. Find a partner or a group. Explore Meet Up, local Facebook or sports Facebook groups. If you can't find what you are looking for, start your own!

3. Take advantage of the free resources that are available at your fingertips, such as YouTube videos for yoga, Pilates, strength training, stretching, Zumba, and more.

4. Commit to it. If you find that you are having trouble fitting in exercise, schedule it on your calendar and treat it like a doctor's appointment that you would not cancel.

5. Find an accountability partner, a person who you check in with about your progress or someone who exercises with you.

6. Reward yourself. Who isn't motivated by money? For every bike ride, run, or yoga class you attend, put some money in your "exercise jar." Then treat yourself with a gift!

7. Pay attention to how you feel before and after exercise. People tend to regret the workout they didn't fit into their day, but you seldom hear sadness about the workouts that people actually do accomplish. So make the time. You will be glad you did.

Chapter 4

Be Creative

"A creative life is an amplified life. It's a bigger life, a happier life,
an expanded life, and a hell of a lot more interesting life."
–Elizabeth Gilbert, *Big Magic: Creative Living Beyond Fear*

Being creative can take on so many different forms. Make playdough.
Write in a journal. Play music. Create art. Write a poem. Knit. Bead.
Paint. Build with Legos. Construct a fort with pillows and blankets in
the living room. Throw pottery. Color. Yes, color. Coloring is not just
for kids. There are mental health benefits that adults can obtain from
knitting or the simple act of coloring with markers or crayons![18] Coloring
has also been shown to reduce test anxiety in college students.[19] Creativity
has been associated with increased happiness and relaxation and decreased
anxiety.[20] As it does not have to take much energy or movement, it has
been shown to be an effective method for helping women emotionally
when they are coping with illness.[21]

The wonderful thing about being creative is that you have total
freedom. You can choose to create anything you want in any way you
want. Producing something in itself is a source of pleasure. You can make
something that you can take apart, such as with Legos or playdough, or
you can make something that results in a beautiful product to be proud

of. That freedom of doing something for pure pleasure has wonderful therapeutic value.

Being creative can take you back in time. What did you do as a child that you gave up because it was "childish," or you did not feel "good enough?" Engaging in a creative act from your childhood can transport you back to that time and make you feel youthful.

Engaging in arts and crafts serve as an escape from the demands of everyday living. When we are creating, we are able to let go of our worries and racing thoughts. We give ourselves permission to quiet the part of our brains that are responsible for overthinking and rumination, which can lead to depression and anxiety. In addition, some crafts involve repetitive motions that become similar to meditation. Many people specifically choose activities such as knitting, crocheting, and beading because the repetitive action decreases stress and anxiety.[22]

Neuroscientist Kelly Lambert, author of *Lifting Depression* states that engaging in crafting results in a mixture of neurotransmitters that make us feel good. This includes serotonin that is secreted during repetitive movement, dopamine as the "reward" neurotransmitter, and endorphins, a pleasure producing endorphin released with exercise.[23]

Crafting on your own has its own value and engaging in a craft with others has added benefits. One study[24] found that the benefits included:
- Mental challenge and problem-solving
- Social connection
- Mindfulness
- Hand-eye coordination, spatial awareness, and fine motor dexterity
- Learning and teaching
- Focus
- Active creativity
- A sense of pride and achievement
- Patience and perseverance
- Increased memory formation and retrieval

I never thought of myself as a creative person, but I have always felt a need to create. At every stage of my life, I can think of one type of art or craft that brought me joy. When I was very young, it was playdough. My mother cooked the ingredients on the stove, and the aroma filled the kitchen. We each got to pick our own color as she put a drop of food coloring into the batch. We had to wait until it cooled down enough so that we could touch it. I loved the way it felt when it was still warm, with pieces of undissolved salt. I would spread it out on the kitchen table and use cookie-cutters to make whatever shape I wanted.

As I grew older, I enjoyed coloring books. I spent hours and hours coloring intricate designs with fine-point markers. The more detailed the design, the better. Then I moved on to latch hook rugs. I sat outside in a chair with silver metal tubes touching the outsides of my legs and scratchy fabric that crisscrossed under my butt. I would sit in that chair with my latch hook kits amongst the lush ferns for hours at our trailer in the Poconos. If I was feeling really adventurous and crafty, I would turn that rug into the front of a pillow. Subsequent crafting endeavors matched the fashion of the eighties, including every preppy accessory I could come up with—barrettes, belts, and Bermuda bag covers.

Decades later, I was a poor graduate student, and my lack of finances dictated handmade gifts of all kinds for any occasion I needed a gift. Hair scrunchies, painted pots and vases, wood crafts with artificial flowers attached with a glue gun—even my wedding favors were handmade. I was so proud of the 150 hand-painted, heart-shaped photo frames with dried flowers glued to them. These also doubled as wedding table place cards to inform guests where they were seated. When I was not in class, I spent hours hand painting each frame in shiny gold and gluing to the frame a tiny bundle of dried flowers wrapped in a raffia bow. Several times I burned my fingers on the metal of the glue gun, and my fellow doctoral students wondered what I was doing in my free time that ended up causing me pain when I tried to type or write in class.

After having children, I wanted to capture memories, so I began scrapbooking. That turned into card making. This kept me busy for several years.

When my children were still quite young, I took an adult class in jewelry making. Twice a month, this helped me to escape the after-dinner madness in a household with a five-year-old, four-year-old, and two-year-old. After learning a few techniques from my class, I quickly became addicted to beading. I made more jewelry than I could ever possibly wear. When I say "addicted," I'm not kidding. I became hooked on the therapeutic benefits of beading.

I began beading at midnight. I would write child abuse reports from my job as a forensic psychologist from 8:00PM to midnight. I could not go to bed with horrible stories of child abuse in my head, so I would bead. Then I noticed that I did not feel right when I did not have the opportunity to bead before going to bed. It became my panacea for protecting myself from the vicarious emotional trauma of writing about heart-wrenching story after story of child abuse. I just knew that it made me feel good. Now, through studying the research, I understand why crafting with a repetitive movement feels so good!

You are never too old to start something new. You will benefit from cultivating creativity in your life and making time for it on a regular basis. For further reading and inspiration on the beauty of creativity, I highly recommend reading *Big Magic* by Elizabeth Gilbert.

Take Action

1. Is there an art or craft that you used to enjoy as a child that you gave up because it was too "childish?" There is no rule book that says that these activities are just for children! So buy or make playdough. Create with Legos or Tinker Toys. Invest in a coloring book.

2. Is there a new craft, hobby, or art that you would like to learn? Many supply stores offer classes, or you could learn through YouTube videos.

3. Check the judgment at the door. There is no room for self-judgement in being creative.

4. Would you be interested in an art/craft that is simply doing, or would you like to see an end product? If you would like an end product, would you like to see it quickly, or would you prefer an activity that takes much time until the final product is created? Answering these questions can help guide your choice of activity.

5. Check your local library for opportunities to learn a new craft or get together with others and engage in a favorite craft.

Chapter 5

Read

"Books are the quietest and most constant of friends;
they are the most accessible and wisest of counselors,
and the most patient of teachers."
– Charles W. Eliot

When I decided to include this chapter, it was because I have memories since childhood of escaping into a good book and feeling content. During my youth, I often relaxed in a hammock at our camper in the Poconos, gently swinging while my feet touched the large ferns all around me as I devoured every Judy Blume book. I especially loved *Are You There God? It's Me, Margaret.* I just thought it was so cool to have my name in a book.

Fast forward to over a decade later, when I turned to reading to help me cope during my fiancé's illness. I read every book I could find related to coping with cancer and treatment. After he died, I was comforted by clinical books about learning to cope with death,[25] as well as the spiritual and metaphysical books related to life after death.[26] I spent hours and hours at the Omega Bookshop in Rhinebeck, New York when I would visit my poet friend Kristen when she lived in Red Hook. Just having those books in my hand provided me with comfort and hope.

When questioned by others about what contributes to my happiness, I always had to mention reading. I knew it helped me with my happiness, but I did not understand why. I knew that reading is such a wonderful escape—a distraction from the demands of daily living.

But I didn't really understand why reading helped me so much until I started writing this chapter and doing some research. I came across several research studies about the benefits of reading, including increasing vocabulary and even increasing one's intelligence quotient (IQ). But I wanted to hone in on the emotional and psychological factors, since after all, that's what this book is about!

One study found a strong connection between reading and feeling relaxed.[27] This study was done in 2009 at Sussex University with Galaxy Stress Research at Mindlab International. The researchers found that reading helped reduce people's measured stress levels by 68 percent. They also reported that reading for just six minutes helped reduce stress. And to my surprise, reading was found to be even more effective in reducing stress than going for a walk, listening to music, or drinking tea!

There are some theories regarding why reading is so helpful in reducing stress. First of all, it involves cognition. In order to read, you have to concentrate, using your brain. This pulls you into a literary world and serves as a distraction from your worries or sadness. But it really is more than a distraction. Reading creates a different level of consciousness, as reading incites creativity and piques the imagination.

Another study found that reading helps with empathy.[28] This is related to happiness because empathy improves social relationships. Psychologists and child development experts say that empathy is one of the most valuable skills for healthy and happy development and success in life. As human beings, social relationships are an important part of life. Empathy improves these social relationships, and those improved social relationships boost happiness.

One particular study found that reading fiction helps with empathy in that it helps the reader understand different cultures and personalities. The authors concluded that we all want to belong, and books provide an outlet for belonging. They help to feel connected to something that is greater than ourselves.[29]

A related article found that reading helps us understand relationships.[30] The researchers found that reading books helps us to understand others. This in turn increases our empathy for others and also increases our ability to make social inferences. One study found that reading helped teens with social engagement. It assisted with personal development by providing insight into mature and healthy relationships and interpersonal interactions.[31] If this can happen for teens, then it can happen for adults too! After all, we never stop learning and growing!

These are important for meaningful social relationships, and having meaningful social relationships in our lives increases life satisfaction.

Reading also has tremendous therapeutic value, both through fiction and non-fiction. In both fiction and non-fiction, we can help resolve problems and find closure through identifying with the protagonist or other character. With nonfiction, we may gain skills and help heal ourselves through both pop culture and books written by experts in the field.

When I was grieving, some of the most helpful books for me were those written by others who had also experienced loss. I was particularly affected by Victor Frankl's Man's Search for Meaning. While I appreciated his message and was deeply affected by his story, his life was so different from mine. I desperately wanted to find a similar book that was current and written by a young widow who had found love again. I knew it was possible for this to happen, but I needed to read about it. Unfortunately, I could not find such a book. So I wrote one, *I Can See Clearly Now: A Story of Love, Grief, and Gratitude*. I hope that my story provides comfort for another young widow who may wonder if it is ever possible to love again, or if she is ready but needs courage to do so.

Take Action

1. Discover your best time to read. For some, this is in the quiet moments of the early morning with a cup of coffee or tea, before others have risen. For others, it's in the quiet right before bed. For others, it's an escape during lunch hour on a busy workday.

2. Take time out to read whatever helps you to escape or grow. This could be romance, suspense, science fiction, classic literature, self-help, or a book of inspirations. Reading has the most positive impact when it is something you truly enjoy.

3. Join a local book club. Most libraries have one. If that does not meet your schedule, or you cannot find one, create one! Or you can join or create an online book club. There is no shortage of booklovers.

4. Find opportunities to volunteer and read to others. Look into libraries, schools, hospitals, other children's groups.

Chapter 6

Listen to Music

"One good thing about music.
When it hits you, you feel no pain."
–Bob Marley

Music is powerful. Depending on your emotional needs at the time, you can choose music to achieve your desired emotional outcome. If you feel that you need to de-stress, listen to some soothing music. One study found that classical music and meditation music were the best types of music to achieve a calming effect.[32] If you need to be energized or need a quick mood boost, listen to music with fast tempo. If you need a laugh, turn on some old classics from the eighties and go back in time. Music affects the pleasure center of the brain.[33] We simply cannot help but react to it. We are wired to do so. Use it to your advantage.

People often listen to music simply because it feels good. And when you learn what feels good for you, you purposefully repeat that behavior for the same desired result. This was found in one study where participants reported that one of the main reasons that they listened to music was for arousal and mood regulation. It's reasonable to think that over time, without even thinking about it, we can gravitate toward coping methods that put us in a better mood.[34]

One study found that people subjectively reported "shivers down the spine" or "chills" when listening to beautiful music. During these times, blood flow changes were noted in the brain regions believed to be involved with emotion, arousal, and reward/motivation. This is the same part of the brain that becomes active in response to other pleasure-inducing stimuli, such as alcohol, sex, and food. This links music with the pleasure and reward center of the brain.[35]

Listening to music also helps with anxiety and stress reduction. One study found that people who listened to music prior to a stressor had better physiological recovery, as measured by the secretion of the stress hormone cortisol, compared to a group that listened to rippling water, and a group that did not listen to any sounds.[36]

Lyz Cooper of The British Academy of Sound found amazing benefits of listening to music.[37] Listening to music helped people to feel relaxed, feel happier, release sadness, and increase focus. Some specific findings included that after listening to music, 79 percent of people in the study reported reduced muscle tension, 84 percent reported less negative thoughts, 87 percent reported that they felt more emotionally stable, 82 percent reported that they felt more peaceful and content, and 91 percent felt relief and release of sadness.

In addition, listening to music with others helps provide bonds between people. Have you ever felt connected to another person while listening to music, and you and the other person have not uttered a word? This is the kind of magic that happens when people enjoy music together. It's why I cry every time I'm at a concert held at my relatives' Methodist church in Haddonfield, New Jersey, where my uncle served as director, my aunt was the organist, and my two cousins sang in the choir. As a relative, I had the privilege of sitting in the front row, with the Philadelphia Philharmonic Orchestra so close to me, I could have reached out and touched them! I felt the bass in my chest. I saw the violinists move their bows in unison with intensity during a crescendo. I saw sweat from their brows, as well as my uncle's, when he turned around to say a few words to the audience. I listened to the contrast of the masculine bass voices with the angelic sopranos. The experience was so incredibly moving, I could not stop crying throughout the entire concert. I thought I was the only one, until I looked across the pew and saw another woman with a tear resting on her cheek.

Listening to music from your past can bring you back in time. Have you ever listened to an old song and then suddenly remembered an event or experience from that era along with the feeling that came along with it? This is powerful stuff. Every time I hear "Dream Weaver" by Gary Wright (1975), it reminds me of my first attempt at a sleepover when I was in second grade. The song was playing on my friend's clock radio, and it made me homesick. I made it until 2:00 AM, and then I just had to wake up my friend Jeriann so that I could go home to my house, just yards away, to be in my own bed, in my own house, with my family. Similarly, hearing "Magnet and Steel" by Walter Egan (1978) transports me back in time to the carefree summer of being ten years old, and I can feel the sticky fabric of the backward facing third row seating of the station wagon under my thighs. Since we did not have seatbelts during those times, that song also gives me the sensation of sliding on the seat just a little bit, as my dad drove the station wagon around corners and bends.

Take Action

1. The research helps us understand that listening to music can actually serve as a protective factor against stress. In other words, you can proactively boost your stress response by listening to music before a stressor. So if you needed a good reason to listen to music, there you go!

2. One way to immediately boost your mood is to listen to music. The research helps us understand that your choice of music is important.

Classical music and meditation music were the most powerful in elevating mood. Upbeat music can also help you elevate mood.

3. Create a playlist of your favorite songs and listen when you need a quick mood boost.

4. Go to a concert! Experience the added benefit by connecting with others at a musical event. This does not need to be a fancy or expensive concert. Check the schedules of your local churches and high schools.

Chapter 7

Sing or Whistle

"I don't sing because I'm happy.
I'm happy because I sing."
–William James

Have you ever heard someone singing or whistling, and that person looked mad? In distress? Probably not. Being in a good mood is often a precursor to whistling or singing. Happiness seems to come first. Happy people whistle. They sing because they are happy. Then I wondered if the reverse is true— can you can elevate your mood if you whistle or sing? You can trick your brain into being happy by putting on a smile. Does the same work with whistling and singing?

While I could not find any research to back up my hypothesis, I'm going to stand by my theory! I believe if you are nervous or unhappy, engaging in the act of singing or whistling will elevate your mood or decrease stress and anxiety. Whistling and singing help to quiet the mind.

With a quick Google search, I did find many essays about whistling. These were written by people engaged in creative writing who provided anecdotal evidence that whistling or singing, whether they wanted to do it or forced themselves to try, helped to elevate their moods when they felt down.

So while it may be true that most of the time, happiness comes first before whistling and singing, several people wrote about elevating their own mood by engaging in these activities. And it works for me too, which is why they made it into this book! Why not give it a try?

Take Action

1. The next time you find yourself spontaneously whistling or singing on your own, or even while listening to music, pay attention to your mood. Most likely, you are feeling pretty good.

2. If you are feeling down, angry, or experiencing unhelpful racing thoughts, try whistling or singing. Do you notice a difference in mood?

3. When you're engaged in a mundane task, such as doing laundry or washing dishes, boost your happiness level by whistling or singing.

4. When you're out walking or hiking in nature, sing or whistle for even more happiness!

Relationships

Chapter 8

Connect with People

※

*"The most important things in life
are the connections you make with others."*
–Tom Ford

Have you noticed a change in your sense of connection with others? Are you spending more with time with technology when you used to enjoy interacting with humans? Do you get sucked into social media with the goal of feeling connected, only to feel disconnected? Well, you are not alone. Studies demonstrate that people are experiencing more loneliness than ever.[38] Social media plays a role in higher rates of loneliness[39] and disconnection, but there are other societal factors as well.

We are social creatures. We need human connection. Studies demonstrate that feeling connected to others is an important factor in happiness. One study found that the quality of close friendships is more associated with happiness than the quantity of friends.[40] Another study found that what contributes most to happiness in best and close friendships is the companionship factor, or spending time together.[41] As technology gets more and more advanced, humans are being replaced by machines. A simple example is the check-out counter at the grocery store or Target. Usually, this is an option. You can choose the aisle with the cashier, or you can choose the self-check-out lane. However, during a recent trip to CVS, I did not even have the option. In both spots where a human being usually stands behind the counter filled with rows and rows of candy and gum was a sign that the check-out station was closed. I had no choice but to use the machine, with a robotic voice greeting me and providing me with instructions.

Before the existence of self-check-out aisles, while waiting online at the grocery store, you may have made "small talk" with the person in front of you or behind you. Then maybe you made "small talk" with the cashier, talking about the weather. And it really is not "small" talk. In fact, it is quite significant talk. It all adds up during the day, making us feel part of a community and connected to the world. I don't mean to sound dramatic, but we are losing our sense of community.

So often, the opportunity for meaningful human interaction is replaced by technology. This is happening not just by replacing humans with machines, but through the interference of personal devices, such as laptops, computers, and smartphones, during social human interaction. People are staring at their phones while out to dinner or during a conversation at a party. People are streaming movies and concerts rather than going out and being with others. People are already feeling more disconnected and lonelier than ever. As this is associated with higher levels of depression, it is reasonable to predict that a greater lack of connection through replacing humans with machines and human interaction with technology will result in greater loneliness and greater depression. It's a high psychological cost on society. The psychological toll of lacking human connection has been exacerbated during a global pandemic. People have had to shelter in place, going without interacting with other human beings in person.

Using technology results in a lack of connection within our households. Partners are having conversations while also sending emails or being entertained by a personal device. One study found that the use of a smartphone diminished the enjoyment of a face-to-face interaction.[42]

Parents are asking their children questions while the child is glued to the smartphone. Sadly, smartphones have distracted parents from developing feelings of connection while spending time with their children.[43] Children are video chatting or playing interactive games on-line instead of having a "playdate" and interacting in person. They are connecting, and that is better than isolating and feeling lonely, but it is not an adequate substitute for our need for in-person human interaction. Studies demonstrate that the best emotional benefit related to happiness comes from good ol' fashioned meeting in person and having face-to-face contact.[44]

During COVID and "sheltering in place," people have looked for other ways of maintaining connection with loved ones outside of their homes. While in-person remains the best way to feel connected, this has been a time when people have used technology out of necessity. Relatives have gathered over weekly Zoom calls. Best friends have had dinner together or watched a movie during a Zoom meeting. As restrictions lift, people have rejoiced in their ability to gather in small groups while social distancing and wearing masks.

So what can you do to maximize the emotional and psychological benefits of your human interactions?

Look people in the eye.

I don't mean look people in the eye in a creepy way. I've just noticed that people don't really look at each other anymore. As stated above, we are social beings, and we are losing connection with each other. We're busy multi-tasking, looking at our phones, being distracted by to-do lists. This lack of connection is leading to a feeling of budding emptiness, or for some, full-blown emptiness and profound loneliness. So look your child or partner in the eye when he or she is talking to you and look the grocery store cashier in the eye when he or she asks you how you are doing. You can really get a sense about someone and make a connection with simple eye contact. Making eye contact releases oxytocin in the other person, fostering connection by producing a feel-good, cared-for feeling.[45] Making eye contact is one of the basic social skills that we teach children.[46] So why aren't we doing it anymore?

Every day make a point to connect with two people.

Reach out to someone who supports you and makes you feel good. Reach out to someone who could use your support. One idea is to scroll down to the bottom of your text messages and reach out to someone you have not connected with in a long time. Connect and reconnect.

Make a plan to get together in person with someone.

As stated above, studies have shown that nothing can replace in-person meetings. Talking on the phone may help you feel connected, texting/email/social media may help you feel connected, but do not let this replace in-person meetings. Call a friend for coffee or a walk and get together! During a time of social distancing, you could choose a location where you're able to sit outside and enjoy a beverage. You could also choose a less-traveled sidewalk or trail wide enough to comfortably walk apart.

Put away the distractions.

It's not enough to make eye contact. In order to be fully engaged with someone, you need to eliminate or minimize distractions. If your child is wanting to tell you a story about school and you are on the computer, don't just look at your child. Close the computer screen. Turn the phone off. Through these actions, you communicate to your child that you are fully present and paying attention.

One study found that simply having a smartphone in sight significantly lowered attention to a task. In the study, the phone was turned off and was upside down, yet it still served as a distraction.[47] So put them out of sight. This applies to the home and out in the world. Cellphone distraction in the classroom has also been associated with lower grades.[48]

Also consider what message you're sending. When you make a conscious effort to put your phone away, you are telling whoever you are with, "You are enough." So next time you are waiting at the doctor's office with your child, resist the urge to whip out your phone. Look at your child and start a conversation. If you are out to dinner with your spouse, keep the phone in your car. One study found that having a cellphone visible while two people were talking made for less meaningful and engaging conversation.[49] The presumption was that the presence of the phone signified that the people could be interrupted at any point during the discussion. This caused them to naturally settle into more trivial topics of conversation. Can you go two hours without being able to be reached? Can you give two hours of your undivided attention to whoever you are with?

Make a point to connect every day with your family.

Everyone is so busy these days. With sports, Scouts, employment, homework, PTA meetings, etc., it is difficult to find the time to spend together. A solution is to see what is already there and to make the most of that time.

For example, many families have dinner together. Studies demonstrate a correlation between family dinners and better mental health and communication skills in children,[50] improved grades,[51] and the avoidance of engaging in teen risky behavior, including substance use.[52] Some suggestions for making the most of this time include keeping electronics off of the table, expressing gratitude, avoiding talking about a problem for one child in front of siblings, and keeping the conversation positive.[53]

Get the most out of travel time.

You could make a family rule that electronics and earphones are not used for short car rides. If it is a "rule," then you do not need to argue about it each time you get into the car. These car rides are the times when we can learn about our children's days and their thoughts. Also, just being together, even in the absence of words, is an opportunity to connect. When our children are plugged in and tuned out on their devices, we miss out on these moments. In order to encourage these talks, you could purchase a conversation starter to keep in the car, such as Tabletopics Family: Questions to Start Great Conversations, which can be purchased on Amazon.

Limit screen time and time on devices.

Screen time, whether it is on a computer, smartphone, or tablet, can be addictive for both parents and children. This type of activity will not only take away from family time, but studies have linked screen time with depression and anxiety. Resist the temptation to whip out the device during spare moments. We have small periods of down time during the day, and we have become so accustomed to being entertained and processing information that we feel the need to fill a void when nothing is happening. We need that free time to unwind, think, process emotions and thoughts, or just be. We need that down time to connect with our children in the absence of distraction. If you need support, motivation, or ideas related to minimizing your phone use, read *How to Break Up with Your Phone* by Catherine Price.

Spend time with your child for five to ten minute every day at bedtime. This is a great time to check-in with our children because it is a quiet time without distractions. This could be an opportunity to talk about your child's day, express gratitude, or just lay down next to your child and be together. At bedtime, children are tired, their defenses are down, and they are more emotionally vulnerable. This can be a time for poignant connecting on an emotional level.

I was blessed to have a wonderful role model for making human connections. My father always spoke with people and ended up making friends wherever he went. While I was a child and somewhat naïve, I assumed he knew all of these people because he acted as if they were already his friends. Well, they may have become friends, but they all started out as strangers. When speaking to others, my father seemed to have an intuitive way of connecting with people and making them feel good. He did not talk about himself. He asked questions about the other person, and he treated everyone with the same level of respect. I witnessed firsthand how these conversations and the connections he made brought him so much joy wherever we went.

My father used to ski every Wednesday during the winter, regardless of the weather. Sometimes he would meet up with friends. Other times, he skied by himself, and he looked forward to all of the different people he would meet riding up the chairlift by being "single" and needing to pair up with people for the chairlift ride. Later at the dinner table, he would talk about the different people he met, simply by connecting with them during a ten-minute chairlift ride.

I was also blessed to see him in action. He connected with strangers by asking them for their first name if they were not wearing a name tag, making eye contact, complimenting them, and saying something silly using their first name that made them laugh. He did this with gas attendants, as in New Jersey you are not permitted to pump your own gas, with ski lift attendants, restaurant servers, doctors and nurses during my hospital stay after knee surgery, Burger King clerks—you name it! These short conversations were not insignificant. He made people feel important. He made people feel seen. And in doing so, whether he knew it or not, he was increasing his own happiness through human connection.

Talk to people.

Make eye contact. I know this can be a hard thing for people to do, particularly introverts. Maybe you feel too busy. Maybe your life feels fraught with problems and difficulties and your minds is spinning so you feel lost in our own world even when someone is right in front of us. Maybe you have social anxiety. Maybe you have experienced trauma in the world. Maybe you're too self-critical. Maybe you care too much what others think. Whatever it is, it is worth examining and addressing to see if you can open up in this way, keeping in mind that the number one factor related to overall happiness in life is human connection, including connecting with strangers.

After I turned fifty, I noticed that I began to care less about what others think, including my own loving family members. Of course I cared about my teenagers' feelings, but I no longer cared if I embarrassed them in public because I talked to a stranger or complimented someone's hair. They might not like it in the moment, but I hope that for the long-term, I am demonstrating to them exactly what my father showed me—the importance of human connection and ways of connecting with others all day long.

Take Action

1. Be introspective and examine what interferes with willingness, desire, and ability to connect with others and make a plan to address it. This could involve a simple shift in mindset and taking action by using some of the suggestions below, or it could involve seeking out supportive psychotherapy.

2. As you go about your day and opportunities naturally present themselves, make something of it. This need not be a long conversation. Remember, "small" talk is important. Smile. Make eye contact. These are the simplest ways of connecting. If someone opens the door for you, look the person in the eye and say, "Thank you for opening the door for me." Ask the bank teller how their day is going. It is totally fine and remains powerful even if the interaction is simple.

3. Create device-free zones. Make a rule not to have any devices at the dinner table in order to minimize distractions and have more meaningful conversations. For short car rides, make a family rule of no electronics so that conversation can occur. Keep devices out of

bedrooms so that you can be more present with your partner and not be tempted to go on your phone as the first thing you do upon waking.

4. When a family member is speaking to you and you are on an electronic, stop what you are doing, and make eye contact.

5. Resist the temptation to take use your device as a substitute for human connection. For example, instead of scrolling on social media, call, text, or write to an old friend.

6. Challenge yourself to connect with one person in a meaningful way, every day. Meaningful need not mean a lengthy conversation. Meaningful simply means communicating to someone through body language and simple words that they are noticed. They are important. In return, you will feel the connection.

7. Reach out to two people every day. This could be via text, email, phone, or an old fashioned letter.

8. Schedule a time to get together with someone in person, even if it is brief. Nothing can replace in-person connection with another human being.

9. Because our relationships are the number one factor related to happiness, I began my monthly membership community, Feeling Good with Dr. Peggy, with the month of January dedicated to cultivating and strengthening interpersonal relationships. In that month, you'll find material related to deepening relationships with friends, coworkers, family members, partners, and even strangers! https://drpeggydelong. thinkific.com/courses/feeling-good-with-dr-peggy

Chapter 9

Compliment Others

*"The happiness of life is made up of minute fractions —
the little soon forgotten charities of a kiss or a smile,
a kind look or heartfelt compliment."*
–Samuel Taylor Coleridge

Giving someone a genuine heartfelt compliment raises the positive energy level of the interaction. If you find yourself having a positive thought about someone during an interaction, why keep it to yourself? Share it, and you will both benefit emotionally. Complimenting others is related to happiness because it fosters our human need to feel connected to others. It's also related to happiness because compliments are a form of giving, and we learned from another chapter, "Give to Others," that giving increases happiness.

Have you ever had a nice thought about someone just pop into your mind while you are speaking to them, and then decide NOT to say anything? Maybe you want to compliment her on the shirt she is wearing. *Oh, she'll think I'm weird or a psycho.* Maybe it is something kind that you heard that he did for someone. *Oh, he'll think I'm being nosy.* Maybe it was her positive contribution to a meeting. *Oh, that was last week. Why should I bring it up now?* The truth is, oftentimes when we have a natural positive thought about someone, there is a counteracting thought that prevents us from saying it. *There is not enough time. It is not on track with our conversation.* Whatever it is, get over it! Almost 100 percent of the time, saying the compliment will elevate the conversation, not take away from the conversation.

When you compliment someone, pay attention to how your compliment changes someone's facial expression. Remember that so many people are fighting private inner battles, and your compliment can make a positive impact that you never imagined! Where you saw sadness or a frown, you may now see a slight smile or a huge grin. See how your words elevate someone's mood. You may see happiness in someone's eyes. Remember that emotions are contagious, and you will feel an elevation too!

Through a simple compliment, you can feel good just knowing that you brightened someone's day. Knowing that you are having an impact on a human being, on the world, can elevate your own mood and help you to feel powerful in affecting change. When we compliment people we know, it reinforces their value in our lives and the world and strengths our relationships.

An interesting side effect of complimenting someone is that it enhances your own well-being. Complimenting someone fosters warmth and makes the interaction more pleasurable.[54] When you compliment someone, you are acknowledging that there is enough of that quality to go around. You are coming from a place of abundance thinking. This in turn helps to elevate your own self-confidence and recognize positive qualities in yourself. When people come from scarcity thinking, they have the mindset that if they compliment someone, it means that the other person has something, and they have less of it. In order to hang on to what they have, they say nothing. Fear keeps them trapped in scarcity thinking.

When complimenting someone, be specific. The more specific you are, the more you are conveying a thoughtful message to the recipient. Instead of, "You look so pretty," try "You look so pretty. Your hair is a beautiful color." Or instead of, "That was a great comment during the meeting," try "I was impressed by your comment during the meeting. You really demonstrated knowledge and insight to get the program going in the right direction." Or whatever. But be specific and be sincere.

There may be times when a compliment does not come easily. Then you have to look for it and find it. But it is worth your time and energy to do so because it is one more way to develop a positive mindset. Finding the good in others helps us to find the good in ourselves. Finding the good in others helps us not just to see the person in a more positive light, but doing so helps us begin to see the world in a more positive light. That makes us feel good, that contributes to positive mood, and that contributes to happiness.

Then the next time you hear some awful story on the news or a horrific post on social media, it does not affect you as much because you are focused on the positive. By looking for the good in others where it's a challenge to find, you are training your brain to see the positive.

Here is a beautiful example of how a simple compliment made someone's day. Last year, I was checking in to a hotel in Government Camp, Oregon. I was exhausted. I had been up since 3:00 AM, flew from Newark to Denver, then Denver to Portland. Then I had to lug my daughter's giant, heavy bag of skis through the airport to the car rental area. I was given a tiny SUV, when I had asked for a mid-size SUV to fit the skis. My daughter and I somehow got the skis to fit, but I was sweating, and my arm muscles were tired and shaking by the time we were done. Thankfully, we had a beautiful drive from Portland to Government Camp where she was attending a ski camp. I dropped her off at her ski lodging, leaving her with the people who run the ski camp. They seemed like capable people, but they were strangers to me. Now on top of physical exhaustion, I was emotionally exhausted dropping of my "baby!"

I parked the rental car in the hotel parking lot, then wheeled my luggage to the lobby. My muscles were so sore, I could barely hold the hotel room door open as I tried to squeeze in with my luggage, as it shut on me too soon. As I wearily approached the receptionist at the front desk of the hotel, I noticed her bright smile immediately. After she gave me my room key, I noticed that my mood had lifted since I walked in, and I attributed this shift to her smile and cheerful disposition. I felt compelled to tell her. I simply said, "I love your smile!" and I walked away, rolling my luggage on the tile floor, hearing it make a thud each time the wheels hit a groove in the tile floor.

I then walked to a different section of the lobby to get a cup of coffee before heading to my room. Don't you just love it when hotels offer free beverages and snacks? While I was getting my coffee, I heard the receptionist that I just met. She did not know I was still there. I heard her say to her coworker, "Did you hear that? She likes my smile!" She sounded so happy, and that made me feel good. A few moments passed as I was putting cream into my hazelnut coffee and throwing away my garbage. Her coworker was wiping down a counter in the lobby, so this cheerful receptionist was now at the reception desk by herself. I heard her say quietly to herself, "That just made my day." I felt incredible that just my four words, "I love your smile," had such a positive impact on her. So simple. So powerful.

Take Action

1. The next time a positive thought comes to mind about another person, challenge yourself to say it. Even if the person is a stranger. Even if you do not know how it will be received. Pay attention to the changes in the other person's facial expression. Notice that you uplifted his or her spirits. Notice how you uplifted your own spirits.

2. Pay attention to any thoughts that are interfering with you saying the compliment. What thoughts are running through your head? Be prepared with a counteracting thought for each thought that is trying

to keep you "safe" by not saying anything. This could be, "Don't keep positive thoughts to yourself" or "Have courage and share your compliments," or "A compliment can brighten someone's day."

3. If positive thoughts about someone are not coming easily, look for them. Find them, and then share them.

4. Pay attention to how giving compliments makes YOU feel! You will most likely experience an elevation in mood. Pay attention to this, fully experience this, and celebrate this!

Chapter 10

Surround Yourself with People Who Make You Feel Good

"The company you keep is the happiness you reap."
–Amen Amare

Did you ever notice how you feel differently depending on your company? Make a point to spend time with the people who make you feel good about yourself and less time with the people who bring you down. Pay attention to how you feel after spending time with certain people. Researchers have coined a term for this experience, "emotional contagion." This occurs when an individual or group influences the emotions or behavior of another person or group through conscious or unconscious exposure to emotional states, behaviors, and attitudes.[55]

Researchers found that happy people tend to be among other happy people. Each happy friend increased the person's probability of being happy by 9%![56] One study found that when people were exposed to positivity, it made them more likely to express themselves positively. Conversely, when people were exposed to negativity, they were more likely to express themselves negatively. It was noted that this was in the absence of nonverbal cues, suggesting that it was solely the emotion that was communicated and felt by the other person.[57]

Trust your gut on how you feel spending time with certain people. Some people are so clever with their insults that you may question yourself and think that you are crazy for feeling bad. Trust your gut. Did someone insult you, and then say, "Just kidding!" after the hurtful words are out of her mouth? Did a "friend" make a joke about something she knows bothers you and then say you're "too sensitive" when you become upset about it? Does a "friend" avoid making eye contact with you when you are out for coffee or dinner with a small group? This is called "relational aggression." Some people are quite good at it. They may try to make you feel like you're wrong or even "crazy" when you call them out on their negative behavior. Trust your intuition and minimize your time with these people. Your gut is trying to tell you something.

In the first years of living in my town, I worked fifty hours a week with three children under the age of four. I was with my children most of the day, and I would work until midnight. I did not have time for meeting people and making friends. I got together for coffee a couple of times a month with a small group of women, and I welcomed the opportunity for adult conversation outside my private practice.

Unfortunately, I noticed that after spending time with these women, I felt worse, not better. What really upset me was the gossiping in this group. The gossiping! I get sick to my stomach thinking about some of the comments they made, telling stories and making fun of other moms. I am nauseous now that I listened to it and didn't stop it. Truthfully, at the time I was relieved because they were not criticizing me. What I didn't realize was that as soon as I left the room, they were talking about me! One of these "friends" liked to tell me about the negative things that another woman said when I was not there. This was worse than anything I had experienced in middle or high school. I recall clearly telling myself that I needed to get away from this group.

I then went to my bookshelf and reread the chapter, "Be Impeccable with Your Word" in *The Four Agreements*, by Don Miguel Ruiz. He explains so well why gossiping is toxic, why we feel worse when we gossip or are around those that do, and to instead focus on speaking positively.

When I was with this group of women, I was not accepted as a woman who earned her doctorate, had a thriving private practice, was raising three beautiful children, and doing a decent job of balancing the work/family thing. This group tore me down. They didn't insult me directly, but at every opportunity, they made nasty remarks about working women while I sat right there with them.

I felt like a schoolgirl who was trapped in a class with a bunch of not-so-nice girls but had to make the best of it because there was no one else around. But I had never actually experienced that in my childhood, and I was having difficulty handling this situation as an adult. All throughout my school years, I was fortunate to have a great group of kind and compassionate friends. In fact, we are still friends after forty years, and we take an annual trip together. I've stayed with them because they are a wonderful group of kind, thoughtful, supportive women who have been there for me to celebrate accomplishments and milestones and cry with me through loss and disappointment. I had no experience coping with this situation of gossiping, nastiness, and maliciously making fun of others. I suppose that at the time, I was so desperate for adult company that being with women who I did not feel good around felt better than being alone.

It took a visit from my lifelong best friend to truly open my eyes. Jeriann and I met when we were three years old and were next-door neighbors for ten years. She has always been like a sister to me, spending so much time at my house with my family that it felt like she lived with us. She has always been assertive, strong-willed, and protective of me. Even though she is only three months older than me, she was a grade ahead of me in school. She also has two sisters who are ten and thirteen years older than her. This led to her being more mature than me, which often resulted in her teaching me and protecting me.

During these times when I was having difficulty with these women,

Jeriann flew up from Georgia and stayed with me in New Jersey for a few days while she was here for her high school reunion in New York. While we were out for a walk on the dirt road near my house lined with horse farms, I told her how I felt around the Mean Girls. I cried and confided about how awful I felt.

"Jeriann, you wouldn't believe how they make fun of other women! The nasty things that they say are so hurtful. And they put down women who are just like me, in front of me. They make subtle jabs about working women not caring about their children. But it's not said directly at me, so I look too sensitive if I say anything."

In her loving, yet no-nonsense voice, Jeriann gave me the most effective advice in just five words: "Time to get new friends." The solution was so simple and obvious, we both had a big belly laugh, startling a nearby horse! Then she went into full-on Jeriann protective mode and so wanted to give them a piece of her mind. That was it. I just needed to hear my best friend of forty-nine years say what was best for me.

As you can see, it's easy to get sucked into a group where you don't belong. The need for social connections and to belong is so strong that sometimes it can lead to making bad decisions. Life is simply too short to spend it with people who leave you feeling drained, negative, guilty, less than, or ashamed.

I'm not saying that you shouldn't give people a second chance or allow people to make mistakes. But—and this is a big but—no one else is going to protect your emotional well-being. You do not owe friendship to anyone who does not support you or who insults you. Of course, you might feel lonely at first, just like I was afraid of feeling in ditching that "friend group." Yet when I was willing to let them go, I opened up time and space to let more appropriate people in. Thankfully, I found them shortly after I left this group; ten years later, they are still my people.

However, this does not mean you should avoid people who are in a bad place emotionally and need your support or friendship. That is different.

Helping others can actually boost your mood. Another chapter in this book, "Give to Others," describes how and why helping others boosts mood, including the research behind this finding. It is a completely different situation when people are not intentionally hurting you or are affected by a circumstance out of their control. Help these people but be mindful of the emotional contagion phenomena and take steps to take care of your emotional and mental health.

It's true that you can be affected by the mental health of a family member or close friend. Just about every time I do a workshop related to living a fulfilling life, someone in the room asks me how she can get her husband to apply some of the principles. Why? The negativity or depression of her spouse is wearing her down. These people never like my answer: You can't. You can't make someone apply strategies that could make them happier if they don't want to. You can live by example, but no one changes unless they want to change. The point is that you can change your reaction to it and be helpful without making it your responsibility to take on that person's pain and "fix" them. But the good news is, just as you are affected by someone's negative mood, that person can be positively affected by your positive mood!

Even indirect or virtual relationships, such as those on social media, can affect your mood, so be mindful of your online company as well. You may become upset by witnessing an argument between people on Facebook, react to the person who spews hatred and negativity, or become sad and physically ill after your well-intentioned friend posts a video about abused animals or a missing child.

Finally, what can you do when you simply cannot get away from someone who you feel bad around? Whether it's the supervisor or colleague at work, your mother, sister, or even your spouse, acknowledge the emotional impact that the person has on you, and then take some steps for self-care.

For example, if your brother is coming over for Christmas and you know that every time you see him, he criticizes something about your life, prepare yourself by expecting that behavior from him. That softens the blow, and you can feel more confident and grounded if you consider how you might respond ahead of time. Will you ignore it? Change the subject? Tell him he is being rude? Self-care includes considering possible responses, playing out in your head where each one might lead, then choosing the best one for your desired outcome.

After spending time with someone who makes you feel bad, take time for an activity of self-care, something that makes you feel good and helps release the negative energy from the situation. Breathe and meditate. Say positive affirmations to counter the negativity. Go for a walk with the conscious intention of letting go of the negative impact.

If the person happens to be your partner, you can still control the level that you allow it to affect you. Understand that your partner's negativity can have a powerful impact on you and make a conscious decision and set your intention that they will not affect you. Understand that you can love your partner without letting him or her bring you down. You can also control your response. Do not meet your partner's negativity with negativity. That will get you nowhere and will not result in feeling better. It might be hard at times, but meet the negativity with kindness and compassion. See where that gets you. For example, if your wife comes home from work and complains that the house is a mess and dinner is not made, instead of complaining about what she has not done, ask her about her day, and if there is anything you can do to make her evening more enjoyable.

Take Action

1. Trust your instincts. Without getting caught up in words or behavior, focus on how people make you feel or just how you feel in their company. After spending time with a particular person or group, do

an emotional "check-in" with yourself. Simply ask yourself, "How do I feel?"

2. You do not owe friendship to anyone who makes you feel uncomfortable, less than, or not good enough. Spending time with the people who make you feel bad about yourself is worse than feeling lonely. Follow my friend Jeriann's advice: "Time to get new friends." Is there anyone in your life who repeatedly makes you feel worse after spending time together? It's important to make the distinction between that person going through a difficult time, such as depression, and that person intentionally hurting your feelings. If the latter, it may be time to reevaluate the friendship.

3. Monitor your use of social media; notice how you feel. Remember that you are not alone if you feel worse after spending time passively scrolling on social media. Most people do. One way to deal with this is to simply consciously limit your use. Keep the phone out of your bedroom so that you are less tempted to go on social media before you go to bed or upon waking. Remove social media apps from your phone. Try "habit replacement." If you're going on social media out of habit to feel connected, replace that habit with calling or texting a friend.

4. If you want someone close to you to have less of a negative impact on you, live by example and consciously intend for the negativity to flow right over you. Since you cannot change anyone else, focus on your behavior. Also, if you remember the phrase "hurt people hurt people," you can understand that someone's negativity is coming from a place of feeling hurt. This will help to foster compassion rather than resentment. Remind yourself not to take the person's actions and words personally. It's about that person, not you. Time to reread the chapter, "Don't Take Things Personally" in Don Miguel Ruiz's *The Four Agreements*.

5. After spending time with a negative person you cannot avoid, engage in activities of self-care, or activities that bring you joy. If you can beforehand, consider how you will react to potential situations and what you will do after the encounter for emotional repair.

6. Foster positive emotional contagion. Look through the contacts in your phone. As you scroll through, who brings a smile to your face simply by seeing that person's name? Reach out to that person. Do this every week, and you will be surrounding yourself with people who make you feel good.

Chapter 11

Ask for Help and Accept Help

"We all understand the importance of asking for help.
Those who achieve big things are the ones
who accept it when it is offered."
–Simon Sinek

We simply cannot do everything we need to do and get through this thing called life without help. Some people view asking for help as a sign of weakness. Either that, or they worry asking for help will be perceived by others as weakness. Get over it! You will be much more fulfilled in your daily life if you ask for help when you need it. The benefits of asking for help are similar to the benefits of accepting help. When you ask for help, you are increasing your happiness by creating time and energy to engage in activities that bring you joy. When you ask for help, you are using your social support network. Studies demonstrate that social support is related to happiness.[58] Accepting help decreases stress, which results in greater life satisfaction.

While the benefits may be the same, the dynamics of asking for help are different from accepting help when it's offered. When help is offered to you, the perception that you need help is coming from someone else, and that can make you feel uncomfortable. When you are the one asking for help, then it has fallen upon you to recognize when you need help. This gets really tricky for the perfectionist who believes she can do it all, or the masochist who must show the world his pain in doing everything himself.

For many, it takes hitting rock bottom to ask for help. For the heroin user, it may be living out of a car and prostituting for her next fix. For the alcoholic, it may be crashing his car into a tree. For the workaholic, it may be the threat of divorce. For the person who does for everyone else but herself, it may take a diagnosis of cancer that brings her to her knees to begin to ask for help.

It's helpful to think of asking for help as prevention, instead of responding to a crisis. We are much better able to handle things when we are not in crisis mode. Also, receiving help feels so much better when we are not in such a terrible state that it's difficult to experience the joy that comes along with receiving that help.

If you still feel resistance, it may be useful to think about your belief system and what thoughts and beliefs may be preventing you from asking for help. What messages were given to you about asking for and receiving help? How were your parents as role models in asking for help? Did they avoid asking for help? Did they accept help graciously? Did they put themselves down for asking for help?

Once you can accept the need to ask for help and begin to practice this step, you will reap the rewards. You will learn that you do not have to do everything. You will experience the strength and confidence that it takes to ask for help. You will feel the joy, relief, comfort, or whatever it may be in receiving that help. And, finally, you will receive the satisfaction in knowing that you provided an opportunity for someone else to feel good about himself or herself by reaching out and allowing that person to help you.

Confession here. I am one of those people who has difficulty asking for help. I don't believe that I'm a perfectionist or a martyr. I just don't want to inconvenience anyone. Or maybe I felt guilty because, for the most part, my life has been manageable.

Within the past two years, I've been practicing asking for help. It's been a wonderful, experience for me as I sought support while I transformed my professional life. In my career, I shifted gears, leaving work that was familiar, comfortable, lucrative, and predictable—yet painful. For fifteen years, I dedicated my professional life to the field of child abuse and neglect, conducting forensic psychological evaluations with families.

After conducting approximately 4,500 interviews where I listened to tragic stories of abuse and trauma, my heart could not take it anymore. I needed to do something different. So I began doing work that heals my soul. I knew it was what I wanted to do, but it was not familiar terrain for me. I had no idea what I was doing. Although I had always run my private practice on my own, I never felt like a business owner or entrepreneur. When I shifted the focus of my private practice and turned to sales, I needed a lot of help. A lot of help. I was excited to be in new territory, but I was painfully aware of my naiveté. I knew I needed boatloads of assistance. Marketing help. Branding help. Clarity help. Training help. Advertising help. Focusing help. Social media help. Email list help. Time management help. Networking help.

I am so grateful that the help was available, and that all I had to do was ask. I joined a women's empowerment group, Believe, Inspire, Grow (B.I.G.), made up of mostly entrepreneurs. I asked, I asked, and I asked. Some women I paid, some kindly donated their time, knowledge, and expertise, and others suggested bartering. All of that help led to the publication of this book! I couldn't have done it on my own, and I'm grateful that I asked for this assistance.

For further reading about asking for help, read Amanda Palmer's *The Art of Asking*. If maintaining an image of perfection is preventing you from asking for help, read Brené Brown's *The Gifts of Imperfection*. If the fear of vulnerability is preventing you from asking for help, read Brené Brown's *Daring Greatly*.

Accepting help increases happiness by freeing up your time or energy to engage in activities that bring you joy. It also increases happiness by decreasing stress. Not only does the help decrease stress, but receiving support decreases emotional stress. First, there's a difference between asking for help and accepting help when it was not requested. You may need to get beyond the self-judgment that an offer means that you appear like you don't have it all together. Here's a little secret: no one does. People may appear as though they have it all together, especially on social media, but everyone struggles with something. This is not to celebrate that others are struggling, but to find comfort that you are not alone. Second, accepting help may feel like you are relinquishing control, especially if it was not your idea. You may not be able to control the manner in which the help is offered. Don't worry. You still have control in how you receive it.

Accepting help may require examining your own beliefs and past experiences that interfere with your ability or willingness to accept that help. What does accepting help mean to you? You may need to get out of your own way and release any thoughts that prevent you from receiving assistance. Assess your judgments about receiving. What do you think it says about you? Do you view it as weak? If so, you need to address that. Also, sometimes our past disappointments and emotional pain prevent us from accepting help. We may become guarded and set up a wall of concrete to protect ourselves from being hurt or disappointed again. If this sounds familiar, you need to address this pattern to be able to accept support from others and to heal.

Be mindful of the assumptions that you make when someone offers assistance. We do not know what is going on in other people's lives. Someone's offer to help may mean something different to them than your perception. There may be more meaning and significance to the other person than we are aware of. For example, someone we perceive as having it all together may actually be offering support as a distraction from her own problem, pain, or sorrow that we know nothing about.

A few years ago, my husband was home after major back surgery. He was completely bedridden for two or three weeks. It was such a depressing time, seeing him in so much pain and unable to care for himself. Even the lights in the bedroom caused him pain. I blocked out how long he was in bed. Our children were twelve, eleven, and nine at the time and going in three different directions. To make matters worse, I was working full-time and had injured my leg, causing great pain while walking and standing. My physical therapist advised me that I would not heal if I did not make some temporary changes, and that included not standing for any length of time. So making meals was out of the question.

A friend knew about the circumstances and set up a meal delivery plan with friends. It was easy for me to accept the help because I desperately needed it, but it was still hard for me to relinquish control over what my family and I would be eating for dinner. People were so kind to make food; I did not want to make any special requests. I had to work on letting others decide what they were cooking and eat whatever they delivered.

I looked at each dinner as a surprise, and that helped me to accept that I did not know what was coming. Some days, we were not even sure what we were eating! At the time, it didn't matter because we did not have any allergies or food restrictions in my family. So we ate the mystery food, including the dish with so much cheese that we could not tell what else was in there. Was that chicken? Cauliflower? Tofu? Didn't matter – it tasted good! We accepted and appreciated every dinner!

When I accepted assistance, I needed to let go of pride and control. I surmised that anyone in my position would need help. But it was still difficult to acknowledge that I was in the position of needing the help. For the first time, I was not able to take care of my family's basic needs. This felt unfamiliar, uncomfortable, and vulnerable.

If you have difficulty receiving assistance, here are some ways to look at it that may ease this issue and allow more happiness in this process. My friend Megan McDowell founded Heartworks[59], an acts of kindness group. She helped me understand that we cannot give to others without judgment if we judge ourselves when accepting it. In addition, refusing help deprives others of the opportunity to feel good through giving. When you say yes to receiving the support, you are providing people the opportunity to feel good themselves through the simple act of giving to another human being. In other words, you are receiving with grace.

Another way to look at it: Life is a flow of energy and love. It goes both ways. Sometimes you are the giver, and sometimes the receiver. You disrupt the flow of life when you decline to receive. It is an ebb and flow that creates authentic friendships and genuine relationships through reciprocation. So don't mess with it.

On another note, be careful about accepting help from people who act like you owe them something. They are the ones who "keep tabs" about their kindness and act as if you are indebted to them. A true favor is done out of kindness without expectation of anything in return. If you feel compelled to do something, instead of returning the favor to the person, pay it forward to someone else. Also, be mindful of people who, in doing something for you, attempt to make themselves appear stronger or better than you. For example, another mother may offer a meal for your family or a ride for your child, but do so in a way that is condescending, telling you that she is helping because she is so organized, and you are not.

You do not need to be Super Woman or Super Man, or Super Mom or Super Dad. If someone offers to support you in some way, whether it be a ride for a child, or a meal if you are struggling, accept the gift. To restate what Megan taught me: We cannot truly give to others without judgment if we judge ourselves for receiving. Allow others the opportunity to give to you and receive the help with grace by expressing gratitude and not judging yourself.

Take Action

1. Before you embark on this new journey, examine your belief system. What thoughts and beliefs may prevent you from asking for help? What did you think about yourself when you received help in the past? Similarly, examine your own beliefs about accepting help. Do you think it means that you are weak or not good enough? Do you feel as though you are relinquishing control? Address these belief barriers and replace them with a healthier perspective.

2. Keep in mind that you are providing others with the opportunity to feel good about themselves. The world runs on give and take. It is off balance if you just give, give, and give. Can you think of examples in the past when someone benefited from helping you? When you practice this step, see if you can see its impact on others.

3. Don't wait for a crisis. Ask for help at a time that is not an emergency, when you can really experience the joy of receiving without being in complete meltdown.

4. Start small. Think of one simple way that you need help, who can provide that help, and how you will ask. Once you have mastered asking for something small, you will feel more comfortable asking for something big.

5. Remember you do not need to keep score! Asking for help and giving help involve a natural ebb and flow. It is not forced. It is not a predictable back and forth. Merely because you asked someone for help does not mean that you cannot ask for help again before you have been able to give help. Life is simply not that predictable and organized!

6. Do you have past hurts or disappointments that are affecting your ability to accept help? It is important to acknowledge these past hurts, forgive who hurt you, and move forward with a perspective of new opportunities of allowing new individuals to give to you.

7. Change your mindset as needed. Through giving, people paradoxically receive, and through receiving, people give. By accepting help, you are still actually giving to others through the opportunity for them to feel good through the simple act of giving.

8. If you continue to struggle with accepting help, look for small ways that you can allow others to support you. Pay attention to how you feel and address any discomfort.

9. Make a commitment that the next time someone offers any kind of help, instead of saying, "No thanks, I got this," say, "Oh, that would be wonderful. Thank you!"

Chapter 12

Give to Others

"True happiness comes from the effort of making others happy.
Give and share your love every day."
–Tinku Razoria

One of the best ways to feel more peace and happiness is to give to others. The overall gains are twofold. Someone benefits from your kindness, time, and/or generosity, and you feel better yourself. In addition, doing for others helps take the focus off of our own issues. Rather than being an act of charity, it reinforces that we all have struggles, and by giving when you can to help make someone else's day a little brighter, your day will be brighter, too.

Psychologists now say that resilience is the "new happiness." Resilience is the ability to recover and grow in the face of adversity. We simply cannot be happy all of the time, as no one is without problems. Instead of pursuing happiness, psychologists are recommending that people build resilience.[60] Resilience involves several factors, including social competence, forgiveness, empathy, autonomy, and problem-solving ability. Guess what boosts resilience? Giving to others. Studies have found that people who give to others have high levels of resilience.[61] It does not need to be fancy, elaborate, time-consuming, or expensive. Simple examples include delivering meals or providing rides for someone going through a difficult time, driving a child for a busy mother who is juggling schedules, or donating to the local food pantry. The possibilities are endless!

Let's go deeper into some of the reasons giving helps our mental health. First, it is a distraction from our own worries and concerns. When we go through a difficult time ourselves, focusing on other people and their needs momentarily takes us away from the difficulties in our own lives; it gives us perspective and a break. This is not to say that we should ignore our own problems. In fact, be careful that you don't use giving as a way to excuse or ignore your own issues. Make sure that you continue to deal with your own problems after helping someone else.

Helping other people makes us realize that we are not alone, especially in the struggles of life. Everyone is dealing with something. Often when we give to others, we realize that everyone struggles and has difficult situations. This helps us to feel less alone in our own challenges.

Most of the time, our giving involves being with other people, either as recipients or collaborators. As human beings, we are wired to be social. These social connections help fulfill a basic human need and boost our mood. A 2006 study at the National Institutes of Health by Jorge Moll found that helping others activates the region in the brain that is responsible for pleasure, trust, and social connection, leading to what may be referred to as the "helper's high."[62] In addition, all these connections help to build our social support network, which in turn helps with resilience. Having people to turn to for support and assistance during times of difficulty helps us to cope during these times. The more resilient we are, the happier lives we live. Life is filled with problems; we can bounce back and feel better when we are resilient. Helping others also leads to stress reduction, which in turn boosts physical health. Rachel Piferi and Kathleen Lawler found that people who gave to others had lower blood pressure, which is associated with lower stress levels.[63]

Here's another benefit: giving to others helps foster gratitude, especially for what we have and what's going well in our lives. People who regularly support others in some way have higher levels of perceived happiness.[64] Another study found that simply giving to others through sending a thank you note to someone improved mental health functioning.[65]

Let's look at some ways that you can give to others:

Give time.

Organize a food or clothing collection. Be a big brother or sister. Mentor a young professional. Visit a senior center or veteran's hospital. Volunteer as a scout leader or through a Parent Teacher Association. Serve on a township committee of interest. One study found that people who volunteered more than once monthly but less than once weekly were 12 percent more likely to report happiness than people who had not volunteered.[66] Another study of 13,000 adults age fifty and over found that those who volunteered two hours a week had more positive affect, optimism, and a sense of purpose in their lives. They also had less loneliness, hopelessness, and depression.[67]

Give resources.

If you have an area of knowledge or expertise, see who needs it. Share your knowledge or talent. Run a workshop at a local library. If you are an attorney, offer your knowledge to a domestic violence shelter or other agency. If you are a mental health professional, offer a free workshop in your community. If you are a landscaper, mow the lawn of someone who is ill or grieving. If you are healthy and able, give blood during a blood drive.

Give love and attention.

Visit seniors living alone in nursing homes. Go to a children's hospital and read to children or play games. Sing at a veteran's hospital.

Give money or goods.

Donate to a Go Fund Me for a person needing help. Donate to the Red Cross after a natural disaster. Take all the stuff you don't use to Goodwill. Elizabeth Dunn and Lara Aknin (2008) found that people who spent money on others had higher levels of happiness. The conclusion was that spending financial resources on others fosters happiness.[68]

After my fiancé died, I felt so much better helping others who were also affected by a cancer diagnosis. As a volunteer, I visited children on the oncology floor of the hospital that was across the street from my apartment. I remember one boy in particular, Christopher. He was three years old, with blonde hair and a smile that melted my heart when I entered his room. He was usually feeling well when I visited, and he enjoyed going down the hall to the playroom, holding my hand as we walked. We played with blocks and cars, and I read books to him. His mother was there most of the time, but she also had an infant to take care of. I spent time with Christopher so that she could rest or spend some one-on-one time with her baby. While it was difficult to see so many children suffering, it helped me feel less alone in my grief and in the sadness associated with caring for someone who is gravely ill. Most of all, it gave me purpose at a time when I thought I had none.

In my grief over losing my father and my fiancé, there was a time where I felt like I meant nothing, even though that was never true. When my fiancé died, I felt as though my future had vanished. Losing my father felt like my childhood was forever gone. I was a lost adult, questioning my existence. Giving my time and love to those children helped me more than it did them.

Take Action

1. What brings you joy? What are you good at? How can you give to others by sharing your joy, knowledge, or talent?

2. Keep it simple. Remember that it does not need to be something big or take huge amounts of time. Sometimes these beliefs prevent people from taking the first step. You can always build upon what you start to do.

3. Which way of giving suits you? If you don't have much money to spare, give your time. If you have a full schedule but have money, provide a financial donation.

4. Don't use giving to others as a distraction from dealing with your own problems. Take a break from them, but don't neglect them. After spending time and energy giving to others, check in with yourself and your own life to see what problems or issues may need your attention.

5. Your way of giving is unique to you, so don't compare yourself to how others do it. Do what feels good to you.

Chapter 13

Create and Nurture
a Strong Social Support Network

"Good relationships keep us happier and healthier. Period."
–Robert Waldinger

As human beings, we are hard-wired to be social. To be connected. Hundreds of years ago, that is what helped us to stay alive. Now we need to remain emotionally connected to others for our well-being and overall sense of satisfaction in life. In fact, happiness researcher Shawn Achor says that social connection is the strongest predictor of long-term happiness.[69]

I am always interested in reading research related to how I can best help my clients and students live their best lives. I often suggest relevant articles to therapy clients to enhance their understanding and growth. I also use this research in my monthly membership community, *Feeling Good with Dr. Peggy*, where I teach methods of cultivating resilience, gratitude, joy, and meaning in our lives. Many articles mention the importance of social support, even if that's not the topic of the article. Studies on coping with depression talk about the importance of feeling supported in order to combat the loneliness that often accompanies depression.[70] Studies on resilience mention the importance of maintaining strong social networks for maximum resilience.[71] In my research for my dissertation involving children with cancer, many articles highlighted that children fared better emotionally when they perceived that they had a strong support network.[72] A common denominator in these studies is social support.

This social support is different from the type of connection discussed in the chapter "Connect with Others." That chapter highlighted the value of human connection, including with strangers, and how these interactions and connections make us feel connected to our communities and the world. This type of support is important for happiness and worthy of its own chapter, as I learned through my research how important it is to connect with strangers. In this chapter about social support, however, I'm talking about a deeper level of human connection. Both are important for happiness. In this chapter, I'm highlighting the value of having people you feel close to. People who "get" you. People who are there for you when you need a shoulder to cry on and also there for you to celebrate your achievements.

In my forensic practice, I evaluated over 4,500 children and adults who experienced child abuse and/or neglect or had been a perpetrator of child abuse and/or neglect. In case after case, the individuals who lacked a strong support network experienced the most difficulties in their lives. They exhibited poor coping skills, ineffective stress management strategies, an overwhelming sense of hopelessness, and an overall lack of fulfillment in life. Their stories illustrated what I had found in my previous research: social support is crucial for mental health.[73]

Unfortunately, people with mental health issues, including depression and social anxiety, have problems that prevent them from being social in order to nurture a support network. Spending time with people helps to foster closeness. People who suffer from depression often lack motivation. This lack of initiative may prevent them from engaging in activities that could foster deeper relationships to build a social support network, such as going out to a party, or calling a friend to get together for coffee or dinner. People with social anxiety may desire relationships but may be so consumed with negative thoughts about being judged or ridiculed by others that they do not act on their desire to have meaningful relationships.

In this day of technology, online support can be very helpful for people with depression or anxiety. People can feel more connected by seeing each other on Zoom or Facetime rather than simply sending messages, emails, or texts. Seeing faces and making eye contact makes us feel more connected and cared for.[74] Technology allows for a connection for people who have difficulty leaving their houses, people who want connections but are anxious in social settings, and people who lack motivation to reach out to others to meet in person. In-person face-to-face contact provides the opportunity for deeper relationships. However, developing meaningful, supportive relationships over technology, particularly where faces can be seen, is better than not having any human connection.

As I mentioned in the chapter "Connect with People," technology can actually make people feel more disconnected and lonelier. This tends to happen when people who enjoy being social replace in-person social activity with online social activity. There simply is no substitute for the benefits of face-to-face human interaction. It is not surprising then that people are reporting the highest levels of loneliness than ever before. Loneliness has become so widespread, common, and painful that England has appointed a Minister of Loneliness to help combat the problem.[75] Stay at home orders during COVID19 have exacerbated the loneliness epidemic. One study found that 50 percent of Americans reported feeling lonely, as well as feeling more unhappy than they had in fifty years.[76] This is not surprising given the changes that interfered with regular in-person activities that foster a sense of closeness and support with the ones we love. In-person contact with those we feel close to cultivates our support network, so we feel the loss or loneliness when we don't have it.

Most programs that combat loneliness, depression, and anxiety help people develop ways of reaching out to others and forming meaningful interpersonal relationships in order to build their social support networks.

Social support networks serve as a buffer for going through any type of crisis. Simply knowing that you have people that you can depend who support you can help you feel better during a time of crisis.[77] When we seek to strengthen interpersonal bonds, we can choose to focus on our intimate partnerships, immediate family and relative relationships, friendships, and/or colleagues. For further reading on strengthening relationships in the workplace, check out Melanie Katzman's *Connect First: 52 Simple Ways to Ignite, Success, Meaning, and Joy at Work.*

Take these simple steps to build or strengthen your social support network.

1. Make a point to reach out to one person every day. Call, email, text, or send a message to one person. It does not need to be anything fancy or elaborate. Just tell that person that you are thinking of him or her. Or you could take it a step further and let that person know what he or she means to you.

2. Have a goal to meet in person with someone at least once a week. This is important, as in-person contact helps to foster closeness. Make as much eye contact as possible, which helps foster closeness by making the other person feel good and cared for.

3. Take a look at what you have in common with others. What shared interest, sport, or hobby do you have? This can help bring people together and feel more natural. This also helps foster long-lasting relationships, giving people a common interest or activity as the "reason" for the gathering.

Sometimes when we are seeking connection, we need to first provide what we are looking for. For example, this is what I often think to myself when I feel that I am lacking. When I want to be heard, I need to be a better listener. When I desire deeper friendships, I need to be a better friend. When I am longing for compassion, I need to be more compassionate.

When I want to feel understood, I need to be more understanding. When I want more connection, I need to create connection. When I want more acceptance, I need to be more accepting. When I want more love, I need to be more loving. It's pretty simple. It starts with me. It starts with you. We need to first be what we are seeking.

Take Action

1. Make a list of all of the people you can contact via phone, text, or email. Then every day, pick one person and contact that person. Make it a meaningful connection. Ask how that person is *feeling*. Has he or she mourned or celebrated anything?

2. Make a list of people you would like to get together with. Make a list of activities you enjoy. Then once a week, reach out to one person and get together in an activity you enjoy. If once a week seems impossible, go for once every two weeks. You can keep it simple, such as going out for a cup of coffee or a drink, or it can involve more planning, such as purchasing concert tickets.

3. Remember that social networks need attention. They need to be nourished, nurtured, and maintained. Don't reach out only when you are in crisis mode. Make it a habit to stay connected.

4. If you are feeling that you are lacking in something, first try to be that for others. It does come back to you. I follow this mantra: "It starts with me." What we put out into the world comes back to us. Think about what you may be missing in your life and then provide that for another person.

5. Remember that a strong social support network is a crucial factor in optimal mental health. In fact, it is the greatest predictor of happiness. It is up to you to cultivate your relationships. The good news is that you are in control, and it feels good to strengthen bonds.

You

Chapter 14

Speak Your Truth

⊰⊱

"Speaking your truth is the most powerful tool we all have."
–Oprah Winfrey

I believe that we cannot truly be happy if we cannot speak our truth. Once, a psychologist presenter at a continuing education seminar said that the saddest situation in her private practice with couples is when one partner does not have a "voice." For example, a woman might not feel comfortable letting her partner know that her feelings are hurt out of fear of her partner's anger. Or a husband does not talk about his dream job or passion out of fear of being called silly or selfish. Indeed, speaking your truth will foster happiness, and not speaking your truth (or not having a voice) will foster sadness. This is because we cannot be truly happy when do not allow ourselves to speak freely about our own thoughts and feelings, or when we are pretending to be something we are not in order to please others, particularly in our own homes.

In order to speak your truth, you need to dare to be authentic. You need to dare to be vulnerable. This takes tremendous courage because in doing so, we expose ourselves to criticism, rejection, and possibly ridicule when we express our true thoughts and feelings. When we are able to be authentic and vulnerable, the rewards are tremendous: You honor yourself by expressing your true thoughts and feelings, and people tend to like vulnerable, authentic people. By presenting your true self, you are showing others your personality, where you stand on various issues, and your emotional life so that they can make their own decisions based on their perception of the "real" you, rather than a fabricated or manipulated version of you. This also helps you. By being authentic, you will attract the right people into your life.

There are many different reasons you get stuck not being your authentic self:

- You want to please people.
- You want people to like you.
- You want to avoid conflict.
- You want to avoid hurting others' feelings.
- You fear the consequences.
- Your childhood beliefs get in the way.
- You have low self-esteem.
- You think it is selfish.
- You want to be perceived as "the good girl" or "the good boy."
- It goes against others' perception of you as a "nice" person.

Even when you begin to speak your true thoughts, feelings, and opinions, some people will want nothing of it. It may ruffle their feathers or rock the status quo. For example, a friend may be resistant when you suggest a different activity when you get together because she is used to always having her way. It may be helpful to be prepared for a reaction if speaking your truth involves revealing a secret, a big change, and/or has a great impact on someone else's life. In these cases, out of fear, other people may attempt to shut you down by

- Invalidating/minimizing/explaining away your feelings
- Ignoring you
- Becoming extremely angry, aggressive, or violent, both verbally and physically
- Communicating that you are a disappointment

When you've had enough of concealing your true self and are ready to change your ways, start paying attention to your unwanted or uncomfortable emotions and sensations in your body. Often, we experience the emotion's impact on the body before we are consciously aware of it. It may show up as problems, such as a stiff neck, headache, stomachache or worse. Pay attention to these symptoms. That physical problem is trying to tell you something.

When you are ready to speak your truth, here's a process to follow:

1. After you become more aware of your feelings related to holding back, write them down. Include thoughts on how not revealing your true thoughts and feelings made you feel emotionally and physically and what you would like to do about it.

2. Plan how to communicate your truth. You may wish to do it in person. If you have extreme difficulty talking, then try writing. Communicating on paper is much better than not communicating at all.

3. Practice what you want to say. Visualize how you would like the conversation to go.

4. Make sure that when you do bring it up, you are relaxed. Meditate or do some deep breathing beforehand.

5. Begin to communicate when you feel calm.

6. When speaking, also take ownership of your feelings. Start with "I feel... ." Don't accuse or blame. The natural reaction when someone feels blamed is to become defensive, angry, and/or shut down.

7. Listen to the other person. While your goal is to get your point across, you will be much better heard when you show respect and receive what others have to say.

8. Even if the situation does not go your way, celebrate that you spoke your truth. Take pride and pleasure that you accomplished a difficult task and allow that feeling of accomplishment to bring you pride and joy.

In speaking your truth, it's inevitable that you will come across rejection. How you deal with rejection will either make you stop speaking your truth and give up your goals, or propel you forward. I cannot stress enough how important it is that you have the right mindset to deal with rejection. Because it will come. Overcoming rejection is part of the road to success and fulfillment. It really is all about perception.

I absolutely love the way Jack Canfield describes rejection in his book, *The Success Principles.* He mentions the "SWSWSWSW concept." This stands for "Some will, some won't; so what – someone's waiting." It's so important to understand that rejection is really just opening the door to THE RIGHT PATH. Next!

Rejection is also a way of determining what is REALLY important to you. How badly do you want it? Keep trying if your gut tells you so. If not, next! And you may come across rejection when facing something you really want, and the word no, or no progress, is simply not acceptable to you. In these cases, trust your gut. Don't give up so easily. While remaining respectful, persist.

While trying to get my inspirational/mental health healing bracelets into more stores, I let everyone know my goal. A couple of friends mentioned one store where they thought my bracelets would be a good match. I had never been in that store, but I thought it must be a good idea if two different people suggested it. So I called and asked to speak to the owner. The owner was not in, and her assistant took the message. I did not hear back for two weeks, so I called again. Still, she was not in, so I left a message. Another two months went by, and still no return phone call. So I called again. Once again, the owner was not in, so I left another message. Each time I called, I had never been told no, so I persisted. I called again, and still the owner was not in.

I happened to be in the area of the store one day, so I decided to bring some bracelets with me, stop in to see what the store looked like, and if I felt it was a good match, ask if the owner was in. Well, right away, I could see why my friends had suggested it. It was a perfect match! So I asked to speak to the owner. She was busy at the moment, but willing to give me a few minutes of her time. So I browsed her beautiful boutique, and I purchased a unique hair clip for a friend's upcoming birthday.

Things were magical when I sat down with the owner. She cleared the table setting at a booth, and I spread out my bracelets for her to take a look. She wanted to hear a little bit about my "story," and as I explained the importance behind the angel bracelets and losing my fiancé to cancer, we both had tears in our eyes. She loved the bracelets so much that she placed my second largest order to date. And to think if I had accepted the lack of a return phone call as rejection!

Something else that is helpful when dealing with rejection is what I call an A.W.E.S.O.M.E. file. Dealing with rejection is tough. I get it! Keeping track of inspirational messages, positive experiences, compliments, and accomplishments can help. Keep it all in one place – on your computer, on your phone. Use this acronym to help you. Write down any time you have demonstrated or received positive feedback about Achievement, Wisdom, Empathy, Strength, Optimism, Motivation, Excellence.

When working with my therapy clients, I suggest to them that they write the experience down as close to when it happens, so that they are able to remember it vividly. I also suggest that they provide as many details as possible, including feelings. Then review it whenever you are feeling beat down. The more details and feelings provided helps you relive the experience and benefit from that positivity.

When I look back on my life, speaking my truth in terms of being my authentic self has been one of the most difficult challenges. In recent years, I decided that I had nothing to lose, and I was going to do something about my desire to do less forensic psychology which paid the bills yet took from my soul and start doing work that fueled my soul.

I have always been interested in positive psychology. Martin Seligman, Ph.D. is viewed as the "Father of Positive Psychology." In their paper, he and Mihaly Csikszentmihalyi defined positive psychology as "the scientific study of positive human functioning and flourishing on multiple levels that include the biological, personal, relational, institutional, cultural, and global dimensions of life."[78] When I reflect on my own life and what helped me get through my most difficult days and create the life I wanted, it involved the power of my positive thoughts, specifically gratitude and the law of attraction. So I began talking with other professionals about my interest in gratitude, the law of attraction, and designing and creating inspirational jewelry. I changed my email tagline to include my workshops and inspirational bracelets. I used to hide this professional side of me out of fear of being discredited while providing testimony in court. Soon I was talking about it and including it on all of my printed material.

I consulted with a colleague, another psychologist, about this shift, and how I could start generating work for myself in this new, positive direction. She suggested that I give talks at local libraries. I had given several presentations in the past, but they were all related to the topic of violence. This was a welcome change to contemplate what I could talk about in the field of positive psychology. I thought about what got me most excited, and it was the topic of gratitude. It was gratitude for a simple cup of hazelnut coffee that helped me get through my darkest days while my fiancé was dying from cancer. I wanted to share the healing and growing power of gratitude with the world.

Naturally I felt energized by sharing and developing my interests, and my speaking engagements increased. Previously I had kept my interests quiet out of fear that I would be judged and rejected, considered weird or too "woo woo," and consequently lose my forensic psychology referrals. Now I'm happy grateful that I terminated my contract to provide forensic psychological evaluations because I've developed a private practice of positive psychology. In 2019 alone, I gave over fifty talks, retreats, and workshops related to gratitude, joy, and the law of attraction.

The moment I decided to speak my truth, I felt the change. I felt powerful and gratified because this is what truly interested me. Those feelings energized me even more to keep on sharing who I am with others. I trusted that in speaking my truth, the right people would stay or be attracted into my life and the wrong ones would leave or not be interested. That is exactly what happened. Consequently, I am more fulfilled in my work than I ever imagined possible, all because I had the courage to allow myself to be vulnerable and authentic in my interests and passion.

Take Action

1. Examine everything you are sacrificing by not sharing your true thoughts and feelings with others. Focus on what you have to gain by sharing it.

2. Take a look at childhood beliefs that may be interfering. These beliefs could be statements like, "That's selfish," or "Women don't do that," or "That's disrespectful."

3. Address the reasons that you may have become stuck in this habit. These may include fear of conflict, low self-esteem, or a strong desire to be liked. Become aware and deal with these reasons.

4 Be prepared for negative reactions from others who do not want you to rock the status quo.

5. When you are ready, follow steps one through eight in this chapter.

6. Reach out to a supportive person in your life who can help you through this process. It could be a family member, friend, or a therapist.

7. Celebrate you.

Chapter 15

Learn to Say No

"Saying yes to happiness means learning to
say no to the things and people that stress you out."
–Thema Davis

Learning to say no is one of the greatest gifts you can give yourself. You can say no to an insult, a request, or a suggestion on how to spend your time. Saying no makes you a happier person by decreasing resentment and creating more time and space to do what fulfills you. Declining someone's request may also involve being courageous and giving up your desire to be liked—by everyone. Politely refusing may require getting over your own thought that "nice" people always say yes. Trust me, you can still be a nice person when you do not say yes to everyone and everything.

Think of it this way: Declining requests that are not in line with the way you want to live your life physically, mentally, emotionally and spiritually leaves room for what you do want to do. In turn, you are better able to serve the world by following what you love with heart and grace.

Turning down what does not serve you also leaves room for others to do what may serve them. Let's say your child's team is having a bake sale. You are the first person that the manager asks to bake because you always say yes. But you hate to bake. However, Timmy's mom loves to bake. So if you say yes to something you hate and take up that spot, you are depriving Timmy's mom from doing something she loves. Make sense?

If you are a person who is always giving and saying yes to all requests, it's going to be really hard at first to say no. Others may be shocked; they may even say mean things about you. Do not let this affect you. I know, easier said than done. Remember, what people say about you has everything to do with them, and nothing to do with you. If you need help with this concept, read agreement #2 in *The Four Agreements* by Don Miguel Ruiz. You're welcome!

But I wondered, is it just me? Or does saying no help improve others' mental health? Research in psychology is important to me. When I am sharing ideas, suggestions, or techniques, I feel better doing so when the method's effectiveness is supported by the research.

One study found a significant relationship between saying no and positive mental health among college students.[79] Mental health functioning was assessed through a self-report measure, General Health Questionnaire, and examined one's ability to carry out normal functions, and also examined the presence of distressing symptoms related to depression and anxiety. The people who said no had higher levels of self-reported mental health functioning.

Learning to say no has been one of the most difficult lessons for me. My habit of always accepting what was asked of me was driven by many things: a desire to be liked, to fit my perception of being "nice," to appear as though I could work fifty plus hours a week, raise three young children, and still say yes to requests.

So I said yes to everything, including to things that did not serve me, I did not need, or drove me crazy. I said yes to the wrapping paper fundraiser when my first-born entered kindergarten. I did not want to be that mom who did not participate, even though I did not need overpriced wrapping paper. I said yes to the school's fundraiser of purchasing frozen meals, even though the small window of pick-up time at the school did not meet my schedule, and I knew my kids would not eat the meals. I said yes, yes, yes, until I had a negative experience where I felt unvalued. I am incredibly grateful for this experience, as it was a true eye-opener and changed the way I handle all requests that come my way.

Some parents were coordinating an activity for children in my county, and one of my children wanted to participate. The planning and the activity took place in the late afternoon. At that time in my private practice, I had a full schedule in the late afternoon. Children came to see me after school. Adults with full-time jobs could manage to schedule a session at that time of day. I knew I could not be available to help out in the afternoons without losing much of my income, and I was unwilling to make that sacrifice. I felt pressure to help, since my child was participating. That pressure came from me. So when I was asked to help out by creating a workbook for the activity, I said yes to assuage my self-imposed guilt.

I offered to make the workbook, even though I don't know anything about graphic design, and I am not very skilled or experienced when it comes to computer software for graphics. On top of that, I hated this task. I dreaded it. After teaching myself how to use Printshop and browsing hundreds of images, designs, and layouts to replicate, it was finished! It looked amazing, and I was proud of it! I had worked on it for hours, then pressed one button, and all my work disappeared. I was so frustrated that I had to create it all over again. Plus, I hated myself for agreeing to create it.

When it came time for the leader to thank all the parents who had worked on the activity. I was not invited to the gathering. Somehow, because I was not available and present when they met those afternoons, my work, time, and effort were disregarded or forgotten.

I vowed then and there that I would never, ever again say yes to something that I did not want to do, simply to please someone else, to be "nice," or to diminish my guilt after having said no to another request. This is not selfish; it is wise. Saying no to what does not serve you makes room for what does. Paradoxically, I probably give even more time and energy now to others, but I do not feel taxed in any way because I say yes to what feels good and fuels my soul. I volunteer my time or knowledge in ways that feel good to me. Learning to say no has been one of the best things I have done for my mental health. I do not feel resentful. I do not feel taken advantage of. I have time to give to others in ways that resonate with me, and I do so with joy, which makes the interaction both pleasurable and meaningful.

Take Action

1. Take a look at your belief system and the thoughts and feelings related to why you say yes. They are not all bad; in fact, some are quite good. Take out a piece of paper and write them down. On the left-hand side, write the reasons you say yes that do not serve you. On the right-hand side, list the ways saying yes does serve you. Make a mental note of the top two or three on each side.

2. The next time you are asked to do something, think about your list. Consider why you are saying yes. Are your reasons on your left-hand column or on your right-hand column? If more are on the left, give yourself a gift and just say no.

3. If you are having difficulty, remember this: Saying no to what does not serve you allows time and space to say yes to all the opportunities that do. You will feel empowered through your own assertiveness. Your mental health will also improve because you will not harbor resentment for doing something you do not want to do, and instead will replace that with joy in doing something you want to do.

4. If that is still not enough, think of this: Saying no to what does not serve you provides the opportunity for someone who is better suited for the task, because it speaks to that person.

5. For those opportunities that you are a yes to, say it with intention. Celebrate your giving heart. Do them with love, grace, and all your might.

Chapter 16

Do Not Compare Yourself to Others

꧂

"Comparison is the thief of joy."
–Theodore Roosevelt

Comparing yourself to others is the quickest way to zap your happiness. You may be very happy with your belongings, achievements, and successes; yet, as soon as you compare yourself unfavorably to someone, your joy disappears. In an instant. Just like that. Gone.

I learned about social comparison in my child development class during the first semester of my doctoral program. In fact, social comparison is actually part of normal development. Social comparison theory, proposed by Leon Festinger, states that comparing ourselves to others is a way of evaluating ourselves and gaining information about our own skills, attitudes, and beliefs.[80] According to Festinger, there are two kinds of social comparison. Upward social comparison is when we compare ourselves to others we perceive as being better than us in some way. This may motivate us to improve to be more like them. However, it may also cause us to feel bad about ourselves. Downward social comparison happens when we compare ourselves to others we perceive to be worse off in some way.

Upward social comparison doesn't have to be a bad thing. In some cases, it may actually be helpful. Noticing the skills and abilities of other people can provide us with feedback about ourselves and motivate us to improve. The problem is when we get stuck and let upward social comparison affect our self-worth, or worse, let it dash our dreams.

I often got stuck in upward social comparison when I was young, but it was hard not to. I grew up in a very affluent town, so I had quite a warped sense of what was normal. My family lived comfortably. I know my parents struggled before I was born when my father first started his medical practice, as I often heard the story of how he only had one nice shirt that my mother washed and ironed every day. If we had any financial struggles, I didn't know it. But I often felt like everyone had more. Way more. I grew up with friends who had not just boats, but yachts and second homes at the beach larger than my house. Kids drove BMWs, Ferraris, and Porsches to school while my father drove a Chevy Citation. The floor was so rusted out that there was actually a hole in it, and I could see the road whizzing by under my feet!

There's nothing wrong with having money. The problem was that when I compared my life to those I perceived had more, it made me feel like a "have not." Boy was I wrong. This is probably one of my biggest regrets, not appreciating what I had because I compared myself to others. I allowed social comparison to eradicate gratitude for what I had and make me feel "less than."

It didn't stop there. Kids at my high school were smart, damn smart! Bernards High School was not only one of the best high schools in the state of New Jersey; it was one of the best in the country. It was common for graduating students to head off to Harvard, Princeton, University of Pennsylvania, and Stanford. I happened to be friends with some of the smartest kids. Even though I graduated eleventh in my class, I felt less accomplished when I compared myself to two friends who made the top ten. I let comparison steal the joy of my amazing accomplishment. What would have been better for me? Simply focus on my own success, be proud of what I had achieved, and have faith in knowing that I had a bright future. Unfortunately, this comparison pattern only intensified when I became a mother. I never considered myself to be an insecure person but comparing myself to other new mothers was a guaranteed way to make me feel "less than." New mothers often don't talk about how difficult it is.

I'm grateful that I didn't have post-partum depression, but my brain was fried. The thirty-six hours of labor followed by sleepless nights caring for a newborn resulted in me living in a fuzzy cognitive fog. I had difficulty breastfeeding, and I thought it was easy for everyone else. I couldn't follow the simple directions on how to use a bottle sterilizer, and I compared myself to other mothers who seemed to have it all together. My sweet firstborn needed to be held every minute, or else she would cry. This meant I often could not shower for three days straight. When I did try to take a shower, my daughter would start screaming after I put her in the bouncy seat right next to the shower stall. More than once I had to jump out of the shower with shampoo or conditioner still in my hair in order to console her. So I simply stopped showering daily! Thank goodness, social media did not exist when I became a mother! I may have compared myself to the mother who not only was able to shower, but was able to put on her makeup, do her hair, and post beautiful selfies!

Since I know that social comparison is a normal part of development, and often continues into adulthood even when we have a pretty good sense of identity, I always assess my clients' use of social comparison. Additionally, I assess their use of social media, because it can be a feeding ground for unhealthy upward social comparison. People tend to post their "highlight reels" consisting of vacations and accomplishments, as well as physical attractiveness through "selfies" that are not even real because they have been altered by the latest beauty-enhancing app that whitens teeth, removes wrinkles, and narrows faces.

A recent study found that passive Facebook use significantly lowered self-esteem and increased depression for individuals who have a tendency to compare themselves to others.[81] Other than the chronic complainers who feel compelled to write about every time they received poor services at a restaurant or were cut off on the highway, most people only post the wonderful things going on in their lives, such as a recent vacation or the birth of a grandchild. This is not to say that their good stuff is not real or not worthy of announcing for celebration. But when we only see their "highlight reels" and not the reality of others' lives (including the bad stuff), we do not get the full picture. Then we begin to feel bad about ourselves because of our daily struggles. Since I cannot go back in time and change my overuse of upward social comparison and its negative impact of making me feel "less than," I want to do my damnedest not to ignore others who do the same. I find myself saying repeatedly, "Comparison is the thief of joy."

Now that I'm older and wiser, I am quicker at recognizing when I am comparing myself to others, and I am better at shifting my thinking to all that is going well in my life. Along the way I realized that I usually compared myself to a perception, a made-up story, a standard that did not even exist, instead of reality. These insights only came with experience. The couple that seemed to have it all together got divorced. The woman who I thought looked down on me lost her beautiful house in foreclosure. Of course, I did not celebrate other people's crises, but they opened my eyes that so much goes on behind closed doors that I don't know about. There's a good reason why that is true: it's none of my business.

Fortunately, I now know that I have the power to control my thoughts. If I realize that I am comparing myself to others, I can shift my thinking. You can too! Freedom of thought is one of our greatest human freedoms. It's not easy to steer away from negative thinking, but with practice, it's possible. Anything we want to improve upon requires practice, which involves focused attention and repetition. For example, I could feel bad because a friend just purchased a new BMW while I'm driving a Honda Pilot with 210,000 miles on it. However, instead of engaging in that social comparison, I can choose to focus on memories of all the adventures that I've experienced in those 210,000 miles. With that simple shift, I can change my feeling in the moment. That is freedom.

Take Action

1. When you catch yourself comparing yourself to others, simply acknowledge what you are doing. Noticing and acknowledging your behavior is the first step. You may be doing this all day long and not be aware of it. So pay attention to your thoughts, behavior, and feelings. Ask yourself if you're engaging in upward social comparison. Are you getting stuck there? Are you using any information gleaned to better yourself, or are you allowing comparison to make yourself feel "less than?" If you find the latter, tell yourself to stop, and think about one thing you are proud of. It may sound simplistic, but it works. Use the little cognitive strategy called "positive self-talk."

2. Instead of comparing yourself to others, focus on yourself and your own goals. If you are reading this book, you're probably old enough to have a good sense of who you are and not need to rely on social comparison to evaluate yourself. Instead of using social comparison to beat yourself up, simply outline your own intentions and goals with your timeline, based solely on your life. Regardless of what is going on with everyone else in the world, what can you do to be your best self?

3. Remember that the use of social media exacerbates the negative impact of upward social comparison. Pay attention to how you feel after being on social media and limit your usage if you notice that you feel worse. Most people feel better when they reduce the time they spend on these platforms.

Chapter 17

Allow Yourself to Feel
Unwanted and Painful Emotions

*"If you don't deal with your emotions,
one day your emotions will deal with you."*
—J. Ivy, *Dear Father: Breaking the Cycle of Pain*

I'm all for positivity, but we must balance that with allowing ourselves to feel unwanted or "negative" emotions, too. This is probably one of the most important chapters for me to write. Because I am a positive psychologist, I am often asked what I recommend that people do with their negative emotions, and if I am in favor of stuffing them in order to remain "positive." That might seem like a logical presumption, since I am typically talking about all things positive. My response is that you need to allow yourself to experience your unwanted or painful emotion and to feel it fully. We often think of them as "negative," but I would like to change that to "unwanted" or "painful." I do not believe that they are "negative," as every emotion is valid, and even unwanted emotions can teach us. This chapter is so important because the positive emotional benefits of implementing the ideas in all of the other chapters in this book will not reach their full potential if you do not allow yourself to feel your unwanted or painful emotions. Think of this chapter as a prerequisite for succeeding in the others.

My parents taught me how to fully experience my emotions. My father, a child psychiatrist, always encouraged me to talk about my feelings, and my mother, was always there to emotionally support me in whatever I had to say. I believe that they strongly influenced me to become a "talking" therapist who believes in the power of addressing and expressing feelings. In my office every day, I experience the therapeutic outcomes of this work. Expressing unwanted and painful emotions allows us to get to the other side and experience joy.

Simply put, we cannot heal what we do not address. Similarly, in her books, *The Choice*, and *The Gift*, psychologist Edith Eger says, "We can't heal what we don't feel." So our sadness, grief, or anger will always linger if we do not acknowledge these emotions. In addition, when we shut ourselves off to our "negative" feelings, we are unwittingly also shutting ourselves off from fully experiencing our positive emotions. The depth that you allow yourself to experience sadness, anger, or grief is in direct proportion to your capacity to experience joy, bliss, and delight. This is a basic premise of Acceptance and Commitment Therapy (ACT).[82] With ACT, people learn to stop denying, minimizing, and avoiding unwanted or painful emotions and start accepting them as appropriate and normal responses to particular situations and life events.

Allow yourself to experience disappointment, anger, frustration, or despair. Give yourself permission to own your feelings and fully experience them. Have compassion for yourself as you would for a friend. When you experience a "negative" emotion, resist the initial temptation to avoid it or push it away. Instead feel it, process it, talk about it, write about it. Ignoring it will not be helpful. Pain is simply a part of life. The goal is to learn from it, heal, and grow. You can turn your pain into a strength by learning from it. There is no cure, but there is healing. It is from our pain where we develop our strengths, passions, and greatest life lessons.

When I discuss this with my clients in my private practice, I often use the visual analogy of a messy room and closet. Think of a teenager's messy bedroom with clothes and other belongings all over the floor. Mom or Dad comes in and asks the teen to clean up her room. Instead of cleaning it up by organizing and putting things in their place, she stuffs everything into her bedroom closet. Mom and Dad come in and compliment her on her room. She knows that she does not deserve the praise because she has not dealt with the problem. It's just that the problem is now invisible. The room gets messy again, and Mom and Dad ask her to clean up her room. Once again, she piles everything into the closet. This happens a few more times, until there is no more room in the closet. Then, on another occasion when her room is messy and her parents ask her to clean it up, she opens the closet door to pack more of her "stuff" in it, and everything comes exploding out, all over the place, leaving her with the biggest mess she has ever seen. She is so overwhelmed by the mess that she does not know where to start, and she cannot make sense of anything or where it belongs.

Well, the similar unwanted catastrophe happens with our emotions. When we do not deal with our feelings, they make a mess of our personal and professional lives. By stifling feelings, we also create disturbance in our inner lives, the turmoil and emotional pain that others cannot see, this overwhelming hurt we unwittingly inflict upon ourselves by not addressing our pain when it naturally and appropriately occurs.

Fear of getting stuck.

Many people are afraid to acknowledge and address emotional pain out of fear of "getting stuck" there. It is helpful to have some coping methods and strategies on hand to assist you with building confidence that you will not remain trapped in those feelings. Know ahead of time what you can do to make you feel better once you have explored these feelings. Then plan time for this activity. This could be exercising, meditating, talking with your best friend, listening to music, etc. If you are addressing some unhealed, traumatic wounds from your past, I recommend that you go through this journey with a supportive licensed psychotherapist.

If I am having a difficult day or need to process some unwanted thoughts and feelings, I first accept and acknowledge their presence and allow myself to feel these emotions. For example, during the initial "lockdown" of COVID19, sometimes I would wake up with a sense of dread. I allowed myself to process my grief related to all of the losses, big and small. This included not being able to touch or hug my mother, terminating my women's walking group after six years, closing the doors of my private practice office in town, my high school senior not having her Prom and all of the other celebrations that come along with graduation, and not getting together with my friends for coffee. When I was ready to move on, after allowing myself to feel and process these emotions on these days, I went to one of my favorite places in nature that always elevates my mood, did some beading to quiet my mind, or went for a run, depending on the nature and intensity of the emotion.

Be mindful of others' reactions and do not let that affect you.

There may be loved ones in your life who may not support the expression of anything negative. They may want to shut you down any time you talk about your anger, sadness, disappointment, or grief because it triggers something within themselves. Or maybe they were taught that it is not acceptable to express or discuss negative emotions. Or maybe they were taught that these emotions are "ugly" and should be kept private. Keep in mind that someone's love for you does not necessarily mean that the person can tolerate your pain. It is a reflection of that person. It is not a reflection of you. Try not to take it personally, but most of all, do not let it interfere with your basic need to experience and process all of your emotions.

Then there are other well-meaning people who may tell you to "be happy," or "It's not so bad," or "Get over it" in an attempt to make you feel better. Despite their intent, these words will not make you feel better. These statements do not validate your feelings; they actually try to minimize your experience. You do not feel better, and you may actually feel worse after these encounters. These people may also be invested in you "getting over it" if they believe that they have something to do with your painful feelings. They can be people who love you and care for you, but, these instances, they are not truly supporting you.

Express Yourself.

There are many different ways to acknowledge and express your feelings. Talk to a trusted friend. Write about it. Find a great therapist. The important thing it to express it and get it out. Think of it as a release of toxins. Unwanted emotions really are poison to our well-being, physiologically and psychologically. In any way you can, acknowledge and express your painful or unwanted feelings. When they are not resolved, they have a way of popping up. Popping up in ways that are: 1) unexpected and catch us off guard, 2) harmful to ourselves and others, and 3) more powerful than the immediate issue at hand. This is because our current state is a compilation of all of our past unresolved emotions. And sometimes this compilation is not additive, but multiplicative.

When I was grieving the loss of my father and my fiancé, many people wanted to help me. They offered countless suggestions to help ease my emotional pain. They tried to take this pain away from me. I know it hurt them to see me suffer.

I intuitively knew that the only way to get through this grief was to face it head-on. So I said no to medication. I know medication can be a lifesaver for some people, but this was not for me. I understand that it is the right path for some, but I simply did not want anything to change the way I felt, including medication that could have helped me to feel better, as crazy as that sounds. I even said no to Reiki. Reiki is a healing technique involving a laying on of hands for the purpose of channeling energy and restoring physical and emotional well-being.[83] While that may have eased my emotional pain to a point that I could have been more functional, I still chose to remain in my grief during this time.

I chose to feel my pain, feel it fully, and process it thoughtfully. I went to weekly psychotherapy. I joined a bereavement group. I talked to anyone who could tolerate my pain. I read. I kept a journal. I listened to music, and I cried my eyes out.

Acknowledging my emotional pain and give myself the space to express it are what allowed me to heal. Notice I said heal and not be cured. I do not believe that anyone is "cured" of grief or anger, or any emotion for that matter. Just like happiness, emotional states are fleeting. However, acknowledging and expressing unwanted emotions allow us to be better able to experience and celebrate positive emotions. The capacity to which we allow ourselves to experience pain is in direct proportion to our capacity to experience happiness and joy.

Take Action

1. The first step is to decide. Simply decide to become more aware of your emotions. The second step is to actually be more aware. This is done by paying attention. Sometimes people may need to go back and simply identify all of the possible unwanted, uncomfortable, or undesirable feelings. You may have done such a good job of pushing them away that you do not even know what they are. So imagine what these feel like: betrayed, disappointed, angry, sad, despondent, frustrated, lost, lonely, grief-stricken, hopeless, helpless, impatient, and anything else you can come up with. The first step of awareness may also involve revisiting your "feelings" vocabulary.

2. Find your preferred method of expression. Is this talking to your best friend? Sharing in a support group? Writing in a private journal?

3. Trust that you will not get "stuck" there. Think of some coping methods you can utilize to elevate mood after you have expressed yourself. You may also be surprised that the act of expressing yourself in itself elevates your mood. A therapist can also help you discover and maximize your coping methods.

4. When you don't feel like dealing with a painful emotion, think of the closet analogy. Remind yourself that you are giving a gift to yourself to address it and avoid a future mess.

5. When you are tempted to ignore your unwanted feelings, remember that in doing so, you are unwittingly shutting yourself off from experiencing joy.

6. As you go through this, have compassion for yourself.

7. If you would like further inspiration, motivation, or encouragement to allow yourself to feel and process your painful emotions, read Dr. Edith Egers' books, *The Choice and The Gift.*

Chapter 18

Journal/Write About Thoughts and Feelings

*"I can shake off everything as I write;
my sorrows disappear, my courage is reborn."*
—Anne Frank

All you need to journal is a piece of paper, a pen or pencil, and your thoughts and emotions. Journaling helps us to process difficult emotions and experiences. Writing down our reactions to what happens during the day helps us to process our feelings and make sense of them, which helps us to release them. Journaling is also a helpful therapeutic activity when we cannot be with others, late at night or away from home.

Some people journal for entertainment. Others journal to chronicle and remember events. Journaling can also be used for mental health purposes. Journaling helps to identify negative thought patterns or "cognitive distortions" and critical self-talk. This is very effective, as negative thoughts are often the root of depression and anxiety. Research has demonstrated that journaling has been effective for reducing symptoms associated with depression[84] and trauma.[85] People have better psychological and physical outcomes when they write about emotional, stressful, or traumatic events, compared to people who wrote about neutral events.[86] Writing about these thoughts, feelings, and experiences exposes people to them, thereby diminishing their power, negative impact, and hold that they can have on people, particularly when people are using denial and avoidance as coping methods.

Journaling can also be used to generate positivity. You can create a journal similar to a collection of A.W.E.S.O.M.E. files (Achievement, Wisdom, Empathy, Strength, Optimism, Motivation, Excellence), or a gratitude journal, as mentioned in other chapters. By actively choosing to write about positive thoughts, emotions, and experiences, you are receiving immediate benefits through a boost in mood, and you are helping your brain to think more positively.

If you have never journaled before, you may be experiencing difficulty getting started. First of all, throw away any thoughts related to self-judgment. This is one place where you can feel completely free of judgment, including from yourself. There is no "wrong" way to journal. You may be inspired by listening to music. You can start simply by thinking about your thoughts and feelings in that moment, or in relation to something that happened that day. Write for yourself and as if no one is going to read it.

Journaling is also a useful tool in between psychotherapy sessions. I have encouraged my clients to use a journal to help them process what we have discussed during sessions, to help them with subject matter to bring up in sessions, and to assist them in learning this method of self-healing when others may not be available. When I suggest journaling to my therapy clients and students in my monthly membership community, "Feeling Good with Dr. Peggy," they are often worried that someone will discover and read their journal. This concern is so great that it often prevents people from engaging in this powerful, therapeutic exercise. We discuss the importance of finding a secure, safe place for your journal. For example, you could purchase a small safe with a lock and keep your journal there. This will give you peace of mind that no one will read it, allowing you the freedom to express your deepest, private thoughts and feelings.

I would like to offer some words of caution. Sometimes when people are journaling about feelings, they can feel overwhelmed by what they wrote. Sometimes thinking and writing about troubling feelings can bring up memories from the past, painful experiences that you may not have thought about in a long time. Be careful not to become too focused on your own inner world where you then ignore your outer world. In order to help you shift your mood after therapeutic writing, it may be helpful for you to schedule time to talk with someone after a journaling session or have some other "feel-good" activity ready to engage in afterwards.

For further reading on the therapeutic and mental health benefits of writing, you may want to read *Opening Up by Writing it Down: How Expressive Writing Improves Health and Eases Emotional Pain* by James Pennebaker and Joshua M. Smyth and *Expressive Writing: Words that Heal* by James Pennebaker and John Frank Evans.

Take Action

1. Purchase a notebook or a blank journal, or simply use sheets of paper. Pay attention to your self-judgment. There is no "wrong" way to journal. You want to make sure you can write freely, so be careful of any thoughts you may have about doing it "right." Let those thoughts go. Remind yourself that it's not going to be judged or evaluated in any way.

2. In order for your journaling to be most effective, make attempts to keep your journal private. You will be more likely to write honestly if you write with the idea that no one is going to read it. You may find that you are more likely to get started, and more likely to write without censoring and from your heart, when you have a solid plan regarding how you are going to keep it private.

3. Think about which way you prefer to write. Do you want to focus on releasing painful or unwanted feelings, or is your goal to focus on positive thinking?

4. If you choose to write about painful or unwanted feelings, be mindful that you may need a mood boosting activity afterwards. If something happens during the day, you could call a trusted friend, listen to upbeat music, or exercise. If it happens before bed, you could think about two things you are grateful for.

5. If you are having difficulty getting started, try listening to music. Find a spot in nature. Think about your thoughts and feelings in that moment or that day. You may also find writing prompts helpful. A simple google search will provide you with some writing prompts.

Chapter 19

Don't Take Things Personally

"Whatever happens around you, don't take it personally.
Nothing other people do is because of you. It is because of themselves."
–Don Miguel Ruiz

Being unattached to what other people say or do is much easier said than done. This means not allowing other people's words or behavior to affect you or make you believe that they have anything to do with you. When you work toward non-attachment, you will be much more fulfilled in everyday living. You will be happier because you will stop thinking that others' bad moods, rude comments, or disrespectful behavior has anything to do with you. People's reaction to you is really not about you. It is about them. People have their own histories, experiences, hurts, and wins. Their behavior is based on their own histories and hurts, not on you. This is a basic premise of psychodynamic theory—that our childhood and past experiences influence shape our personalities and have a great influence on our functioning in our adult lives.[87]

Road rage is a perfect example of people believing that a stranger's behavior has something to do with them. Let's say someone cuts you off on the highway. That person doesn't know you and is not out to get you. Generally, that person is not intent on making you mad. You could have been in that person's blind spot. The person could have been an inexperienced driver. It could be someone rushing to get a sick child to the hospital. All these reasons have nothing to do with you.

People who believe that others' behavior has something to do with them also tend to do so on the road and perceive other drivers' behavior as a personal attack. Since they feel violated, they must retaliate.[88] The problem escalates, and two strangers who don't even know each other may end up getting hurt in an accident or killed. One study found that teaching aggressive drivers to restructure their thoughts regarding situations that made them angry while driving significantly reduced their aggressive behavior behind the wheel.[89] In other words, if you imagine that a driver is speeding and passing you on the right on the highway because he is a first responder and trying to get to the scene of an accident, rather than having anything to do with you, you will be less likely to retaliate with aggressive driving.

I believe that not taking things personally is easier to do as you get older, because experience teaches you that another person's behavior is not about you. You may even learn years later that someone's negative behavior that you thought was about you had absolutely nothing to do with you. When you have the benefit of this knowledge, it helps understand the concept. Of course, some situations may make this more challenging, such as being in a co-dependent relationship or having frequent interactions with a narcissist.

I will share a story about how I allowed someone else's behavior to affect my well-being and self-esteem. When I was about thirteen years old, I had a huge crush on a boy. We knew each other for about two or three years, meeting at around age ten. We laughed and skied with a large group of kids, boys and girls, and we were all friends. I only saw him on winter weekends, when I had the pleasure of skiing with our gang of teens in the Poconos. Soon, I joined the mountain's freestyle team, and he was a Junior Ski Instructor at the mountain. Despite wearing the same blue jacket as all of the other Junior Ski Instructors, I could always spot him with his blonde hair! His amazing skiing ability also made him stand out on the slopes. I was drawn to him. He was cute, funny, a great skier, and we got to know each other as young, silly friends.

I went to school seventy miles away from the mountain, and as my crush on him developed, I wrote his name all over my brown-paper-bag-covered textbooks, daydreaming of the upcoming weekend and skiing around him again. Soon, he started to clam up around me. We would ride the chairlift together, and he would not say a word. This boy who I thought was my friend now seemed uncomfortable riding the chairlift with me.

Then came a time where he not only appeared uncomfortable, but I was so hurt when I perceived him as being mean. One weekend on our way to the mountain, my father's hot coffee spilled on my foot. I was late getting into the car that morning, so I got into the car barefoot and holding my socks. Before I could get my socks on, the coffee mug spilled as my dad drove around a bend, and the piping hot coffee immediately blistered my foot. As I was injured and could not ski that weekend, my sister had all my friends sign a card for me. My crush signed it, but he ended his note with "hatefully yours." I was devastated. I thought this was a fourteen-year-old boy's way of telling me to "get lost."

I didn't see him much in high school, and then I went away to college in Vermont. When I returned home to work on my master's degree, I went to this same ski area and hung out at the local dive bar, "The Dump." After not seeing him in about six years, he spotted me across the room, and I could see his jaw drop. He quickly walked over to me and gave me a hug.

"You look great!" he said.

I blushed. The fourteen-year-old in me remembered the giddiness I felt while writing his name all over my books as I looked forward to the weekend to see him while skiing.

"You know," he said, "I always regretted writing 'hatefully yours' on that card your sister had us sign. When you burned your foot. Remember?"

"Yeah, I remember burning my foot." I didn't want to acknowledge that I also remember his awful words on the card.

He continued, "I thought you were really pretty, and I wanted to ask you out. But I thought you must have had lots of boys after you at your school. I was a jerk. I had a crush on you, and I didn't know how to handle it. So I was mean to you. I didn't want you to have any idea how I felt at the time, so I wrote 'hatefully yours.' I'm sorry."

"Oh my God!" I exclaimed as I shifted my feet on the sticky floor of the bar. "Then I suppose you did not pick up on that I had a crush on you, too! Just ask anyone from my eighth grade. I wrote your name all over my books!" We both got a good chuckle, poking fun at our younger selves.

My poor adolescent self didn't know how to NOT take things personally, and I let HIS uncertainty cause ME to feel insecure. Part of me was happy to hear this, and part of me was angry. I was angry at him for treating me that way and for hiding the way he truly felt. I was angry at myself for allowing his behavior to make me feel terrible.

As I have come to learn as an adult, it was my own fault for letting his behavior affect me. In The Four Agreements, Don Miguel Ruiz refers to allowing someone else's words to have a negative impact on you as "poison." It truly is. When we understand that someone else's behavior does not have anything to do with us, not only do we spare ourselves from hurt feelings or more fodder for low self-esteem, but we also avoid the need to defend ourselves, or worse, hurt back.

The first time I read Ruiz' book, I was so excited about this concept and the prospect that it could alleviate some emotional suffering. As a sensitive person, I often found myself emotionally wounded by others' actions. I decided to put it to the test the next time I took something personally. At the time, my son was about to have his sixth birthday party, and I needed a final count for the facility hosting the event. One mother had not responded, so I emailed her to see whether or not her son was coming. Instead of just saying that her son was not able to attend or that he had a prior commitment, she said that her son was going to their classmate Stan's (changed name) party. My son was invited to Stan's party as well, and it was on a different day; so her response did not make sense.

Maybe I'm old-fashioned, but I was raised that you don't talk about parties unless you know the other person is invited, too. I found her response so incredibly rude, it made me want to respond with even greater rudeness! Instead, I took a deep breath and told myself that her rudeness had nothing to do with me. I reminded myself that I didn't even know this woman, and vice-versa. How could her rude behavior possibly have anything to do with me or my son?

So I responded with kindness. I wrote that there must be some mistake, because my son was going to Stan's party as well, as it was on a different date. If she wanted to look at her calendar again, she could let me know by the end of the next day if her son could attend, and that we'd love to have him. I added that if her son wasn't able to attend my son's celebration, we should get them together for a play date. Immediately I received an email back that not only could her son come to the party, but her son had been asking her to set up a play date with my son.

We had them over the next week. The boys had fun playing outside on the playset, while the mother and I sat at my kitchen table over coffee and watched them play. While I never developed a close friendship with her, and our sons were never close, it was a pleasant time for all of us.

This situation could have had a completely different outcome. Or (since we mothers are protective of our children), I could have thought that my son must have done something to this woman's son to make her treat me that way. While I initially felt the need to defend myself and be rude back, that response would only have made things worse.

Now it was fairly easy to understand that her rudeness had nothing to do with me because we didn't know each other. It is much harder to do when someone who knows us well says something hurtful and we take it on. It takes great strength and lots of practice to shift the habit and recognize it isn't personal. But it is possible.

When someone insults you or does some other hurtful behavior (that you interpret that way), let those feelings remind yourself, "Do not take this personally, smart self. This is about her, not me. This is about the way she sees the world, not me. This is her problem, not mine." You are then protecting yourself emotionally, and over time with practice, developing immunity to intentional and unintentional hurtful words and behavior of others.

You may also take it a step further and understand that often someone's hurtful words stem from feeling hurt themselves. You know, that saying, "Hurt people hurt people." Then instead of turning anger into neutrality, you could use it as an opportunity to experience something positive—to feel compassion. This not only frees yourself from hurt feelings, but you can turn it around by experiencing the wonderful feeling that you get inside when you have compassion for another human being.

Take Action

1. If changing this habit is challenging, don't worry; it is for most people. Remind yourself that this is not easy; it will take effort and practice, every single day. Give yourself some slack about how hard it is at first. Re-read this chapter and the chapter "Don't Take Anything Personally" in Don Miguel Ruiz's *The Four Agreements*.

2. When you first notice that you are getting worked up about someone's behavior or words, that is your cue for some self-talk. Simply tell yourself, "Do not take this personally. This is not about me. This is about them. I am okay." Or if you want to inject some humor, think to yourself, "Not my circus. Not my monkeys."

3. Don't wait until you are in the moment to address this common habit; be proactive. Put little signs around your house or put sticky notes in your car. You can write the serious mantra, "Do not take things personally," or the silly one, "Not my circus. Not my monkeys." Or if you want to keep it private and in code, write "DNTTP," (do not take things personally), "NAM" (not about me), or print out an image, serious or funny, associated with this mantra.

4. Another way to be proactive is to use positive affirmations, such as "I am impervious to other's hurtful behavior. I am aware enough to understand that others' hurtful words are not about me. It's about them."

5. Start the day with a brief meditation or deep breathing. Set your intention for the day to practice not taking things personally at every opportunity.

Chapter 20

Forgive

"To forgive is the highest, most beautiful form of love.
In return, you will receive untold peace and happiness."
—Robert Muller

When you hold on to grudges and fixate on the wrongdoing of others, this ultimately only hurts you. You end up being the one carrying that negative energy. I love the saying, "Hanging on to resentment is letting someone live rent-free in your head." When you allow yourself to forgive others who have wronged you and hurt you, you are allowing yourself to heal. It is not easy to do, so consider it a strength and a gift to yourself. Forgiveness is related to resilience.[90] In other words, being able to forgive is an important factor in being able to move on, bounce back, and grow after a perceived wrongdoing or interpersonal conflict. Building resilience is a worthwhile endeavor, as it has been directly associated with happiness.[91] We all face problems and crises in life. When we are able to not only bounce back, but also learn and grow, we are happier and more satisfied in life.

But . . .

Forgiveness is difficult. Why is it so hard to forgive? Part of the reason is that it is hard to forget. Research demonstrates that we tend to remember events and experiences to which we have a strong emotional reaction.[92]

Simply put, we remember situations that are emotionally impactful, where our emotions are aroused.

Thankfully, we do have the power to forgive. Forgiveness is a choice. It takes energy, effort, and time, but it is possible. In fact, in many situations, forgiveness is the very thing that heals us from pain and helps us move on. We are not able to control others' behavior, but we can control our own actions and reactions.

Sometimes people have difficulty forgiving because they believe that it is a sign of weakness, as if it is saying, "It's OK that you did that horrible thing to me." It may be helpful to think of the act of forgiveness as a strength, NOT a weakness. Instead think of forgiveness as sending the message, "I refuse to be associated with your actions. I refuse to be connected to your hurtful behavior. I refuse to let your behavior continue to affect me." This is important, because when we hang on to the hurt, harbor resentment, and refuse to forgive, we risk taking on the worst characteristics of the person, the same characteristics we seek to cut out of our lives.

The first step is understanding and believing that forgiveness is even possible. The next step involves an intention to forgive. Here are some points to consider:

Consider your own anger.

It is difficult to make progress toward forgiveness if your level of anger is high. Take steps to address your anger. This could involve deep breathing, meditation, and other relaxation exercises, talking to a trusted friend, writing your feelings, or consulting a professional.

It is never helpful to meet anger with anger or to meet hate with hate. If you are still having difficulty releasing your anger, it may be helpful to sit down and write a letter to the person you want to forgive. Write down your angry thoughts and feelings toward this person, but don't send it. Instead, rip it up, all the while imagining that you are also releasing the angry words on the paper. It sounds corny, I know. But sometimes this type of symbolic activity is quite helpful.

Consider other feelings and previous hurts that this situation has aroused.

When we feel hurt, it often brings up past pain. It is important to address these memories as well. If past hurts have not been adequately addressed, it tends to have a cumulative effect, with each hurt taking on the pain of the past.

Consider the other person's situation.

Cultivate empathy. While there may be no excuse for the other person's behavior, understanding the other person's situation may help in achieving your goal of forgiveness. As the saying goes, hurt (emotionally wounded) people hurt people. How has that person been hurt? Often, when people intentionally hurt others, it is because they are feeling hurt. This understanding can help take the sting out of a situation. You no longer have to take it personally, and you can start to look at these situations with compassion.

Keep in mind that it is truly in your best interest to forgive.

So if you are finding it hard to forgive for the other person's benefit, remember that it is truly for your benefit. Holding on to anger and resentment takes a toll on your psychological and physical well-being.[93]

Forgiveness does not mean accepting or condoning the behavior that hurt you.

It is simply making a decision to not let it continue to affect you. Forgiveness is not saying what someone did to you is acceptable. It is simply releasing the hold that it has on your well-being.

Put your mental and emotional energy toward reaching your goals in positive ways.

Stop replaying the hurt in your mind and replace it with positive ways of coping with the situation to achieve your desired outcome. One way to do this is to focus on the positive around you. Make a conscious effort to look for compassion, kindness, love, and beauty in other people and your environment. You may also benefit by looking at the situation from a different angle, and that is, "What can this experience teach me?"

Pay attention to your benefits of forgiveness.

Notice any reductions in anger, stress, and anxiety. Become aware of how this feels in your body, and in your heart. Celebrate these good feelings

Consider that you may need to forgive yourself!

Are there any behaviors for which you still have not forgiven yourself? Are you still holding on to shame in any way? If you need some further work related to shame or forgiving yourself, I suggest some amazing books by Brené Brown, *The Gifts of Imperfection* and *Daring Greatly.*

If you are having difficulty forgiving, you may be inspired by the stories of incredible forgiveness in this book, *The Gift of Forgiveness*, by Katherine Schwarzenegger Pratt.

Take Action

1. Address your own anger first. If your anger level is still high over being hurt or wronged, you are not going to get very far with forgiveness. So take some steps to release that anger. Do what works for you—meditate, go for a run, talk to a friend.

2. Focus on the benefits that forgiveness brings YOU. It really is a gift to yourself.

3. Practice forgiving yourself first. You may find it hard to forgive others if you still have not forgiven yourself regarding issues from your past. Think about a time from your past that still carries some shame, regret, guilt, or embarrassment. Say to yourself, "I forgive you."

4. While there may be someone that is occupying your thoughts now related to a conflict that is more recent, consider your past. Is there anyone from your past that if you choose to forgive, you will be freer to forgive others? Think about a time from your past when you felt disappointed, betrayed, ridiculed, or bullied. Say out loud as if speaking to that person, "I forgive you."

5. If you need some assistance in your mindset about forgiveness, read or listen to the words of Pastor Nadia Bolz-Weber in her YouTube video – "Forgive Assholes."

Chapter 21

Know That the Toughest Days Will Pass

"Tough times never last, but tough people do."
–Robert H. Schuller

Difficult times can feel like they will go on forever and never get better. If you can develop the faith that things will change and improve, you can lift your spirits during difficult times.

Looking forward to better days ahead does not take away the pain of today, but there is power in holding on to hope for the future. It's healing to know in your heart that life will get better. Even if things get worse before they get better, keep trusting that the day will come when you will feel better. You may have to repeat to yourself all day, "This will pass. Tomorrow is a new day." Every day is a step closer to a positive shift.

You can use this strategy to get through any difficult day, month, or year. When I was in graduate school, I disliked one of my field placements, and I needed to continue working there for an entire year. That felt like a long time, but knowing that there was a definite day where this ended helped me get through this experience. I also focused on the reward I would receive by completing this work: each day brought me closer to my doctorate. Believe me, sometimes the days were so unpleasant that I just had to focus on getting through the day or even the hour.

I had a supervisor who never called me by name. My name that year was "DeShort." I knew that it was going to be a difficult year working with him when he commented that he could tell that I did not wear foundation make-up on my face, and that he liked this more natural look on women. This supervisor was very bright, but he was also condescending. When we offered our comments, he rolled his eyes. He criticized us in group settings in front of our peers and physicians. He made fun of my academic training at my university, often stating that it was not as rigorous of a program as his doctoral training and dissertation requirements. It would have been easy to feel stupid. I focused on being kind, learning as much as I could, ignoring the supervisor's rudeness, and looking forward to my last day!

Sometimes it is hard to think about positive outcomes in terrible situations. But if you allow yourself for a moment, just a moment, to recognize the newfound strength that you've developed from these experiences, you may gain confidence and feel proud about your growth. Trust that what you are going through is making you stronger and more compassionate and understanding. It's an opportunity to know deep down that you have these qualities, and that you can draw on them during any future difficulty. This is what I found myself continually reminding my clients during COVID-19. When mothers were exhausted after a day of homeschooling their young children with no preparation, education, and training to do so, I found myself continually reminding them of the rock stars they were. They demonstrated strength they didn't know they had.

In general, people tend to feel depressed when they believe that they don't have control over a situation.[94] This contributed to many people feeling depressed during COVID-19. The lack of control that people had over what was happening in the world created a feeling of helplessness. In addition, people experienced a loss of control over their own lives, families, and businesses during this time. This was a clear example of how previously well-functioning people experienced a significant drop in happiness and life satisfaction through loss of control.

If you have some control—over anything—exert it. If you need inspiration or support, talk to someone who can provide that for you. When we feel out of control, we can help ourselves feel better by taking action, even if it doesn't impact the overall outcome. Even if you do not have control over a situation, you may have a better perspective about it tomorrow. You do have control over how you think about a situation. Sometimes just knowing that and exerting that power can help you feel better.

What's more, thinking negatively about the future is wasted energy and only fuels anxiety.[95] It also causes stress and worry. It is filled with "what ifs." The bottom line is we simply do not know the future, so any time spent worrying about it, unless that is prompting you to take positive action, is precious time lost when we could have been doing something more productive or pleasant.

Instead, spend that mental energy focusing on the present. What can you enjoy in the moment? If you have difficulty thinking about something positive, get basic. Focusing on the present keeps the mind from wandering and thinking awful thoughts and helps to decrease stress and worry. For instance, put your attention on something that is pleasing to your eye. Focus on someone reaching out and showing love. Concentrate on the taste of a favorite beverage.

You can also shift your thoughts (and hence your feelings) from worrying about the future to planning what you can do now to bring about the most desired outcomes. For example, if you are feeling uneasy because you have a large project at work, you can outline steps that you need to take each day as you work toward your goal. For example, during COVID-19, I had to shut down my private practice. With that freed-up time, I decided to learn new technology skills, gain required continuing education credits, and teach myself about topics of interest, including neuropsychology. In this way, I significantly diminished any worries and anxieties about the future.

You can learn to focus on the good that shows up in a terrible situation. This can feel tough. It may not seem right to try to find something positive out of a tragic situation. But you will feel better if you can find even one good thing that has come out of what first feels devastating. It may be the support and love shown by those around you. It may be a recognition and celebration of your inner strength. Finding something positive in a tragic situation or life challenge takes a lot of effort, so if it doesn't feel right today, let it go and try again another time. In the meantime, take care of yourself. Make a point to do something enjoyable every day, even if it is only for five minutes, and even if you have to force yourself to do it. During these times, self-care may feel impossible to do. You may have lost motivation. You may feel like you don't have time, or you don't have energy. Your physical condition may have changed.

But there are many ways of taking care of your emotional needs. One of them is to talk to someone about what you are going through. Call a trusted friend or consult with a professional. When I was going through a crisis, I spoke with anyone who would listen. At the hospital, I sought out the social worker. After my fiancé died, I processed my grief with a psychologist and joined a bereavement group. I sought out comfort with every friend who could not simply tolerate my pain, but those who welcomed expression of my pain. Acknowledging your feelings is an important way of taking care of yourself. This is simply because we cannot heal what we do not acknowledge and address.

Another way of caring for your emotional needs and managing stress involves exercise or meditation. Sit down in a comfortable chair and do some deep breathing. Or listen to a guided meditation. Do yoga or go for a walk, run, or bike ride. Take a relaxing bath. Whatever you do, it should be something that makes you feel more relaxed when you are finished.

I came across an insightful blog written by Christine Hibbert, Psy.D.[96] She wrote about a program that she designed to help people get through difficult times. She calls it TEARS: Talk, Exercise, Artistic expression, Recording emotions and experiences, and Sobbing. Each component has its own therapeutic value. When combined, it is an effective way to support yourself, process, and heal. Some may feel uncomfortable with the sobbing part. It doesn't need to be intentional crying. But when the tears come naturally, don't hold them back; let them flow. Holding tears in can be toxic. Emotional tears have been found to release toxins from the body.[97] In addition, it is cathartic and healing when you allow them to roll down your cheeks.

Take Action

1. Repeat to yourself that this situation is not forever, and better days are ahead.

2. Celebrate what you are gaining and learning from your difficult experience. How are you growing? Who is showing you love and care?

3. Exert control somewhere. What small thing can you control? If you cannot control anything, how can you shift your thoughts about it?

4. Resist thinking negatively about the future. Engaging in a positive future-oriented behavior can help. Write down one goal for your future with two actionable steps that you can take toward that goal. Then take those two steps.

5. What simple act of self-care can you engage in today? Get more sleep? Exercise? Watch something funny? Connect with a good friend? Relax?

Chapter 22

Know What You Can and Cannot Change

"God, grant me the serenity to accept the things
I cannot change, courage to change the things I can,
and wisdom to know the difference."
–Reinhold Niebuhr

It is important to recognize and accept the things we cannot change. Why spend your energy worrying about or trying to fix the things you simply cannot change? Being able to recognize this will leave you with more energy for what you can change. In turn, by spending less time on what you cannot change and instead focusing on what you can change and ways that you can improve your life, you will increase your potential for happiness.

We cannot change other people. People waste so much energy trying to change other people. In almost every workshop that I conduct, people ask me how they can change a family member. And they don't like my answer—you can't. You can't make your husband more helpful, romantic, or whatever. Instead, focus on yourself. You can change yourself if you want to, and you can change your reaction and behavior to others.

We also cannot change the unfortunate situations that happen to us. We cannot change a car accident. We cannot change a loved one's death.

We cannot change being fired. We cannot change a romantic break-up. But we can change how we cope, react, behave, heal, and grow.

Some barriers we can change, and some we cannot. The tricky part is knowing the difference. Sometimes even when we think that a rule or a barrier is permanent and we should just accept it, we can change it. So instead the saying "I accept what I cannot change" should really be "I change what I cannot accept!" Know yourself and know what is important to you. If you come upon a barrier that is preventing you from achieving a goal, you do not necessarily need to accept it. You can change it.

Feeling that we do have control over things and then exerting that power or control is a factor in resilience. People who are able to take control over their problems, or at least how they react to problems when they cannot change the problem, are more resilient.[98] People who are more resilient report more levels of happiness than others.[99]

This is related to internal locus of control verses external locus of control. You want to build up your internal locus of control. When something happens, pay attention to your thoughts about it. If you do well on a test, is it because you studied hard (internal locus of control), or is it because you think the professor created an easy test (external locus of control)? Internal locus of control means acknowledging your power, owning your power, and using your power. It means not giving credit to other people or situations, when you deserve the credit.

I am grateful that when I was little, my parents taught me to fight my own battles and solve my own problems. This generation espoused a different philosophy of parenting, a more "hands off" approach that is effective in building character and resilience. Having to deal with problems yourself provides you with valuable experiences to be able to discern when you cannot change a situation, and when you can. Knowing when you cannot change a situation helps you to accept it sooner, and be able to move through the related feelings, such as disappointment or frustration. It is just as important to know when you can change a situation.

One situation that I did not like, but I knew that I could change, occurred when I was on my own for the first time at college. I had to exert my control to get out of an unhappy dorm situation. I was the only freshman living in a large dorm of sophomores. I hated it. No one was mean, but no one was interested in getting to know me. Having already completed a year of college, these sophomores all had their own friends. I was so homesick and lonely already, missing my family and high school friends terribly. Being placed in a sophomore dorm and feeling like an outsider made it so much worse. Rather than wallowing in my sadness and believing that I was stuck there, I decided that this was something I could change. Despite being told that the campus was overcrowded and there were no rooms, I persisted. Every day, I looked into what I could do to have my room moved to be with other freshmen. It took almost the entire first semester, but before I went home for Christmas, I had my new room in a freshmen dorm.

Take Action

1. When you find yourself unhappy with a situation, think to yourself, "Can I change this?" If you truly believe that you cannot effect change, then you need to focus on how you respond. Then that will be where you find your power.

2. If you find yourself thinking that you do not accept something, think about whether you can change it. Can you say with conviction, "I change what I cannot accept?" If so, then do it!

3. Find little ways every day to build up your locus of control. It may change depending on whether something was positive or negative. Pay attention to your thought processes and how you attribute the outcomes of situations. When you have a positive resolution, do you take full credit and have a high level of internal locus of control?

Do you credit others? When things go badly, do you maintain that internal locus of control and believe that you can make change, or do you blame others and give up your power?

4. Don't give up if you want change. If something is really bothering you, and everyone tells you that you just have to accept it and stop trying to change it, follow your gut. Listen to your heart. Sometimes, well-meaning people will try to get you to give up because they want to protect you from the pain of failure. Or maybe they will try to convince you to give up on a goal because they gave up. It may be hard for them to imagine your goal as achievable due to their own failure to achieve a goal, not following their hearts, and giving up.

Chapter 23

Change the Way You View the Things That Bother You

⤛⤜⤛

"If you change the way you look at things,
the things you look at change."
–Wayne Dyer

It is true that we create our own realities. Life is really all about perception. A positive thinker can look at a difficult situation and immediately see opportunity and feel energized. A negative thinker may look at that same situation with a sense of dread and doom and would rather stay in bed in the morning. So, if you don't like the way your thoughts are causing you to feel, then change your thoughts. I know, I know—that sounds way too simple. However, it is possible, and it is a worthwhile endeavor.

This chapter is different from the chapter, "Know That the Toughest Days Will Pass" because in that chapter, I encouraged you to consider the future and recognize that a difficult situation is not forever. This chapter focuses on the present, showing you how you can have a more positive feeling and outcome when you change the way you view something you're facing in your life. When we're able to see situations in a more positive light, it increases our happiness. This is how something previously viewed as an obstacle or annoyance becomes an opportunity for learning and growth simply by changing how you think about it.

First let me introduce a very basic concept of cognitive psychology. Our thoughts influence our feelings and our behavior.[100] If you want to change an unwanted feeling or a behavior, the easiest way to intervene is to start with the originating thought. For example, I often felt anxious when I was a college student. . With self-reflection, I discovered that the feeling of anxiety was coming from the thought, "I'm going to fail this test." I then worked on changing this thought, reminding myself that I was doing all I could to do well on the test by studying and preparing. The test was simply an opportunity for me to demonstrate this knowledge. I want to emphasize that this did not just happen one time and then anxiety was magically never an issue for me anymore. Like many ideas in this book, it took practice. I repeatedly had to address the issue, and each time I did, I felt better, and I performed better.

Similarly, I often felt uncomfortable in new social situations. I had difficulty participating in a conversation because I thought, "I have nothing interesting to say." The task then became changing these thoughts. Instead of putting pressure on myself to come up with something interesting to say, I changed the way I viewed the situation. I looked at each new social situation as an opportunity to get to know someone by asking questions. This is something I continue to do when meeting new people. By taking the pressure off myself to come up with something interesting to say, I feel more relaxed. By focusing on getting to know the other person, I make a more meaningful connection. It's a win-win, all just by changing my thoughts.

This process may be challenging in the beginning, particularly if you have difficulty with becoming aware of your thoughts and then seeing the connection between what you think and the resulting feeling. But with training and practice, we can become adept at this process and experience the positive impact on our emotions.

For me, piles of laundry can trigger negative thoughts. "Why doesn't anyone else do the laundry?" "Why does everyone let it pile up for me to do?" "I am unappreciated and being taken advantage of." When I notice these thoughts, I quickly change them to make myself feel better, and it works every time. Instead, I think, "I am so lucky to have four family members to fill this laundry basket." "I am fortunate to have the money to purchase these clothes." "I am grateful that my children can play sports and get these clothes so dirty." "I am so glad that I have a washer and dryer." Instead of allowing negative thoughts to fester and lead to frustration, recognize the negative thoughts and flip them to positive thoughts. Doing so cultivates a positive feeling. The situation has not changed (the laundry is still there), but perception about the situation has changed. It works like a charm.

Another way to change your thoughts is to look back on a time when things were worse. This intensifies the meaning and the positive outcome. Let's take the laundry as an example. The reason I can so easily shift my thinking into feeling fortunate that I have four people who create piles of laundry is because I used to do my fiancé's laundry, and I missed doing it after he died. I went from doing a load of his clothes every week at my parents' house during our Sunday family dinners to staring at the last outfit he wore in a pile on the floor. His last hospital stay was unexpected, and he never came home. I never did another load of his laundry. With his death came the end of the chore of doing his laundry. This is why I am able to view washing family members' laundry as a privilege. It does not have to involve a loss for you to shift your thinking now, today. You can simply choose to think differently about it.

Make it your intention to discover what a negative thought is trying to teach you. "My daughter won't put her socks and shoes on when it is time to leave the house, and this makes the family late all the time!" The lesson could be that it is simply time to slow down and being late is not the end of the world.

"Ugh! I broke that glass. I loved that glass. I will never find one like it." The lesson might be to focus on relationships and experiences, rather than objects.

"The house is so dirty. I am never going to have time to clean it. And if I do, it will just get dirty again." The lesson might be to be grateful to have family members that make the house messy, and to cherish those people.

"Ugh. I am such a terrible mother. Answering work emails from home when I should be spending that time with my children." The lesson is that you value mindful parenting.

"My hairdresser canceled on me. I really need to get this rat's nest on my head cut." The lesson here might be to be grateful that it is simply the inconvenience of a missed appointment related to appearance and not your health.

"I can't believe she didn't invite my son to the party." The lesson might be to practice not taking things personally.

"I hate my job." The lesson could be if that "hate" is strong enough, maybe it is time to make a life change and look for a new job.

"I have to pay $10,000 to fix the roof." The lesson may be to focus on gratitude that you have a home, and that your home has a roof.

Of course, some situations are just so terrible that you cannot possibly find anything to learn, or at least not at the time. Let those go, and trust that there will be a time in the future when you can revisit them. Also, have self-compassion and don't judge yourself for not being able to identify the lesson during times of intense emotional pain.

Take Action

1. What kind of a thinker are you? Pay attention to your thoughts during the day. There are so many kinds of negative thinking patterns or distortions. Check out an article I wrote, "12 Major Types of Cognitive Distortions that Can Zap Our Happiness" that you can find on my

website here: https://drpeggydelong.com/12-major-types-of-cognitive-distortions-that-can-affect-mood-and-behavior/. Identify which of the twelve most common cognitive distortions you engage in. That will help increase your awareness, which will help you to recognize when you are actively using that cognitive distortion, so that you can do something about it.

2. To help you "do something about it," take a sheet of paper and draw a line down the middle. On the left-hand side of the paper, write down the cognitive distortion, or negative thought. Then on the right-hand side, transform that statement into a positive thought. For example, "I got a D on this test. I am going to fail this class" might be on the left-hand side. Then you can transform this on the right-hand side to "I got a D on this test. I am going to have to work hard the rest of the semester, and I am smart and can bring it up to a B." The more you intentionally practice flipping your thoughts like this, the more likely you will begin to do so automatically, and then more positive behavior that is in line with your desired goal will follow. Although any sheet of paper will do, I have a worksheet that I use with my monthly membership, Feeling Good with Dr. Peggy. This activity that I call "The Flip-It" is available on my website, and you can download it from here: https://drpeggydelong.com/12-major-types-of-cognitive-distortions-that-can-affect-mood-and-behavior/

3. Help train your brain to see the connection between your thoughts and feelings. Take the same list that you wrote in exercise #2. Under the left-hand side, write down how each thought makes you feel. For example, receiving a D on a test and thinking that you are going to fail the semester may leave you feeling hopeless, depressed, and/or unmotivated. The thought on the right-hand side, where you can get your grade up to a B, may leave you feeling optimistic, encouraged, and motivated.

4. With every frustration or annoyance, let those unwanted feelings be a trigger to ask yourself, "What can I learn from this?" "How can I look at this situation differently?"

Keep in mind that this takes time and practice, and it is ongoing. It has taken years for you to develop your maladaptive thinking patterns. It is going to take time and effort to challenge and undo them. But it is possible. As long as you believe that you can change, are motivated, and are willing to put in the work, you can change your thinking. And guess what? You will feel better!

Chapter 24

Use Your Imagination

"Imagination disposes of everything; it creates beauty,
justice, and happiness, which are everything in this world."
–Blaise Pascal

Visualizing your goals is important because doing so 1) keeps your goals front and center, 2), focuses your brain by utilizing the reticular activating system (RAS), the part of your brain that helps you notice and pay attention to what is in line with your goals, and 3) brings you closer to the right people and opportunities to help realize your goals. One concrete activity to assist with visualization is to create a vision board. Cut out pictures and words that represent your goals. This helps you to keep a mental image of your goals in your brain at all times, helping you throughout the day through behavior and decisions that consciously and unconsciously bring you closer to your goals.

John Assaraf, author of *Innercise*, and Dr. Shannon Irvine, neuropsychologist, talk a lot about the power of our thoughts and our brains to influence our realities, and that this is backed by neuroscience.[101] To learn more about this, you can go to www.myneurogym.com, and/or follow John Assaraf on Facebook and Instagram, and listen to Dr. Irvine host The Epic Success podcast.

Keep in mind that when visualizing, you do not need to have a mental image if you do not have one. The visualization can be a "sense" or a "feeling." Visualization can be about anything. This can be to ask for guidance or to be clear on a goal, if you are uncertain. You can focus on what you specifically want personally or professionally, or this can be a more general visualization of abundance, healing, or prosperity.

Visualization sounds complicated, but there are really only four basis steps, as outlined by Shakti Gawain in her book, *Creative Visualization*: 1) Set Your Goal, 2) Create a Clear Idea of Picture, 3) Focus on it Often, and 4) Give it Positive Energy. Visualization was really powerful in my own life. At first, when I read about it, I thought it was a little weird and to "woo-woo" for me. But I was also at a time in life where I was willing to try anything. So I followed the suggestions for visualizations in her book.

I came across the book at the perfect time. I'd processed my fiancé Scott's death as best I could and dated all of the "safe" men. I was ready to live. To me, living meant loving a partner again. Thank God Scott had taught me that was possible. But there was a problem. Having known him, I knew what real unconditional love was. I could settle for nothing less. I had to get serious about what I wanted in a relationship.

Gawain wrote about the Universe responding to energy levels and wanting specifics. The more detailed you can be about listing your desires, she wrote, the easier it is for the Universe to deliver. So I carefully prepared for my creative visualization exercise. Along the way, I second-guessed myself, felt crazy, got my hopes up, and then smashed my own hopes. But I did the damn exercise, anyway: I made my list. Since I was looking for a man, I listed all the qualities I wanted in a life partner:

Intelligent

Employed

Sense of humor

Good looking

Physically fit

Loves the outdoors

Loves children

Wants at least two children

Is not intimidated by my intelligence or frustrated by my lack of common sense

Loves to bike

Loves to ski

While visiting my dear friend Kristen, I picked up some incense in nearby Woodstock. I thought I was hip buying incense—and in Woodstock, of all places! I purchased "Nag Champa," a light and airy fragrance of Indian origin. A combination of frangipani (plumeria) and sandalwood, Nag Champa is often used to purify an area, for meditation, and when seeking spiritual enlightenment. It seemed like a great choice for my visualization exercise. Also, Kristen often burned Nag Champa at her house, so the aroma reminded me of the love of her family.

List in hand with incense burning, I sat on the pink carpet of my childhood bedroom and asked the Universe to be kind and deliver this man to me. Over and over, I stated each quality in my mind and out loud.

"Please, Universe. I'm ready. Send me love. I'm ready now." Maybe it is a coincidence, but I met my husband a few months later. Or maybe I can believe Einstein – "Coincidence is God's way of remaining anonymous."

With imagination and visualization, anything is possible. If you can imagine something and hold it in your mind, you are more likely to make it happen than if you can't imagine it. Imagining and visualizing something brings it into your consciousness, even if what you are imagining does not actually exist in your life. Imagination is a way to expand upon our existence and reach our goals. Reaching our goals is related to happiness.[102] One study found that visualizing one's life and goals in the future and then writing about them improved mood.[103]

Another way that you can improve your mood is to use your imagination to visualize a positive experience.[104] This could be a favorite place or favorite activity. Think about each detail that you can remember and try to involve as many senses as possible. What did you see, hear, feel, taste, smell? Using this method is also an effective way of reducing physical pain. One study found that 89 percent of children with abdominal pain felt better after using guided imagery. They missed less school and engaged in more social activities.[105] Guided imagery was also helpful for adults with arthritis and other rheumatic diseases.[106] This is an important finding, as pain is associated with depression.[107] By utilizing visualization, people with chronic pain have been shown to experience less pain, and they are likely to achieve greater happiness in life.

Many have found that they can tap into their imagination more easily and vividly with aerobic exercise. So if you are having some difficulty getting your imaginative juices flowing, try some vigorous exercise. Go for a bike or a run.

Now, there is some caution among psychologists regarding the use of imagination. If overused or misused, it can be viewed as a maladaptive method of escape, of dissociation. I am not suggesting using imagination in this manner. While imagination can be used as a form of distraction as a temporary reprieve from one's problems or physical or emotional pain, it should not be used in the extreme toward dissociation or chronic distraction as a complete escape from your problems.

When I work with clients who have experienced loss, many think that they will never be happy again. When grief is raw, people experience difficulty imagining that it is possible for them to ever feel happiness again. Imagining that happiness is possible is a prerequisite for it actually happening. Think about it. If someone is stuck in the thought that being happy again is not possible, the person will look for everything around to confirm that belief. This is known as confirmation bias. Then when the person remains unhappy, it is like telling oneself, "See, I told you so!"

Children are really great at using their imagination. They create imaginary friends, and they think they can fly. They imagine that they can do and be anything. Somewhere along the line, the world tells them that their imagination is foolish. "No, that can't be," "You can't have an imaginary friend," "That's nonsense. You're just using your imagination." Then slowly, this wonderful ability that we have to effect change simply by our thoughts is diminished. We need to do better and cultivate and celebrate children's imagination as well as our own in adulthood.

I had the benefit of learning about the power of imagination in a clinical, academic setting. As part of my graduate school training, I worked with children with cancer. My supervisor taught me how I could help children cope with physical pain simply by helping them to use their imagination. He was an international expert in pain management in children, and skilled in the use of hypnotherapy. When he was with the children, he used hypnotherapy and also taught them self-hypnosis to manage their pain.

I was assigned to work with a sweet girl about ten years old. The chemotherapy was causing nausea and stomach pain. I walked into her room, unsure of what I would see. Despite her pain and nausea, she was sitting upright, watching television while playing a handheld video game. She greeted me with a bright smile.

"Hi Suzanne," I said. "My name is Peggy. I hear you're experiencing some bad stomach pain and nausea and that you've been throwing up. I'm here to help you with that. Are you willing to try something that will help you with your pain and nausea?"

"Sure," she said. "I'll give it a try. As long as it does not involved taking more pills."

I moved closer to her, and I saw pictures of what appeared to be her friends on her wall. I stood by her bed where she could hear me clearly, but not too close, as I was a complete stranger.

I told her, "No pills! The cool part is that this is just using your imagination. How neat is that?"

"What do you mean?" she said. "How can my imagination help my pain go away?"

"Well, it's really quite simple. I will guide you. While you are closing your eyes, I will tell you what to imagine. Your imagination then works as distraction, resulting in you feeling less pain and less nausea."

"I'm not so sure about that," Suzanne said, "but I'm willing to give it a try."

"OK. Before we get started, I would like you to get into a comfortable position. Can you get your bed to tilt back a little bit more so you can rest your neck and have your head resting on your pillow?" She reached down and pushed some buttons that helped her to recline a bit.

I took out a piece of paper out of my pocket that I had folded into quarters. This had the five-minute visualization script on it. I encouraged her to close her eyes, then I read the script slowly that guided her to relaxing her body. I then introduced the visualization exercise, which guided her to imagine her favorite scene, thinking about its full detail, using all of her senses.

I felt so powerless that first session, encouraging her to imagine her favorite place, using a script and suggestions provided by my supervisor, the expert. Suzanne did not report any reduction in pain after our session, and I felt defeated, like a failure. I was not successful in helping her reduce her perception of pain.

My supervisor sent me back to see her the next day. I tried something a little bit different. Rather than simply instructing her to use her imagination and think about her favorite scene, I guided her through that scene. So in a way, I used my imagination, said out loud what I was seeing and feeling in my imagination, and encouraged her to see and feel it, using her imagination. She stated that her most peaceful place was the beach and boardwalk at Point Pleasant, New Jersey. Thankfully, this was a place I was familiar with, so I described it for her in detail, and encouraged her to visualize it. I said, "The sky is blue, with puffy white clouds. The water is clear, and you can see the seashells and creatures on the ocean floor.

You step on the wet sand, and your feet sink deeper and deeper with each wave. Then a large wave comes and hits your leg, splashing ocean water up onto your face. It cools your warm face, and you taste the salt on your lips. You see and hear the seagulls, circling the children with food the beach. Then you smell their food, funnel cake, and it makes you hungry! So you walk slowly out of the ocean, feeling as though each wave is pulling you as the water goes back out to sea."

I celebrated a small victory, as she reported one point lower on the pain scale. She was no longer reporting an eight on a scale of zero to ten, but now a seven.

And I returned the next day, and the next day. Each day, I started off introducing ideas from my imagination, using everything I knew about this particular beach and boardwalk, and slowly she was able to do so without my words and just her imagination. By the time we were done working together, she reported that by herself, when her pain spiked to an eight, she was able to get her pain level down to a three, just by using her own imagination. I felt like a million bucks, but I really hadn't done anything. I simply re-introduced her to the power of her imagination, bringing her back to about age three or four when imagination was everything.

Take Action

1. Keep it simple. Using your imagination is not rocket science. Whatever you are going through that you are not happy with, imagine it gone. Then imagine what it would feel like with it gone. Even if you do not believe it at first, imagine it. Remember that the first step in creating reality is that first we must be able to imagine it.

2. Keep in mind that this works best when you are emotionally ready. It just might not be the time to move on yet. And that's OK. Take time to grieve your loss. Experience the pain of a breakup. Experience

the fear of job loss. Just don't get stuck there, and when you are ready, begin to imagine how you would like your life to be.

3. It's OK if it takes some outside help to get started. This could be a trusted friend, or the assistance of a professional, such as in psychotherapy. You may need time and space to heal in order to create space for imagining. For some, it may be helpful to listen to a guided meditation before imagining on your own.

4. It may be helpful to think about yourself as a young child and how easy imagination came to you when you were so little. You are the same person. That imagination is still there. It just needs a jump start. It just needs to be re-awakened. You can get started by imagining your favorite place when you were a child. Visualize the scene and all the colors. What do you see? What do you hear? What do you smell? Can you picture yourself there? Can you feel yourself there?

5. If you need some help in this area, try one of the many apps, such as Calm, Insight Timer, and Stop, Breathe, and Think. Or read the books Into the *Magic Shop* by James Doty, MD, and *Innercise* by John Assaraff. Then try some of the exercises in their books. You may also benefit from listening to Shannon Irvine's podcast, *The Epic Success Podcast*.

Chapter 25

Smile

*"Smile in the mirror. Do that every morning and
you'll start to see a big difference in your life."*
–Yoko Ono

I love the saying, "The greatest accessory you can wear every day is your smile." Smiling engages people. It makes you appear more likable and approachable. This perception is important because as human beings, we are hardwired to be social. Studies demonstrate that people who self-report being social have higher levels of happiness.[108] Having a strong social support network can serve as a buffer during times of stress. This is known as The Stress Buffering Hypothesis and has been supported extensively in the psychological literature.[109]

On the flip side, not having a social strong support network can make a person feel worse during a time of crisis. This is why therapists often encourage people who are feeling depressed to join a support group and find other ways to develop meaningful relationships. Feeling connected to others improves mood. As I've mentioned before, it's not about the number of relationships, but the depth of them. Having a close relationship with one or two trusted people is far more powerful than having a surface relationship with 100. It may seem overly simplistic to say if you want more meaningful relationships to just smile, but this just may be the very start you need. It sets you on the path for a positive interpersonal interaction, and interpersonal relationships contribute to happiness.

I will never forget when a high school friend, David, told me that before he got to know me, he thought I was unapproachable and snobby, a real bitch. The summer before my senior year of high school, we spent a week at the New Jersey shore together. The magnificent house that my friend's parents rented was right on the ocean. I was a guest of my friend Elizabeth, and David was a guest of Elizabeth's brother. We were in completely separate groups in high school due to the two-year age difference. But at the beach, we were all together. The age and grade difference didn't matter.

David was quite handsome, and extremely intelligent. I was delighted for the opportunity to get to know him. Every night after dinner, this group of girls entering senior year and group of boys entering sophomore year would hang out together on the beach. We had different activities during the day, but every night, all week, we would congregate on the beach after dusk and listen to music and talk.

One night on the beach after dinner, David and I were listening to and watching the undulating surf while listening to James Taylor sing "You've Got A Friend" on the boom box.

"I'm pleasantly surprised how nice you are!" he said.

"What? What are you talking about? Why in the world would you be surprised?"

"Your face in homeroom. Your frown. You look like you can't be bothered. Like you don't want anyone to talk to you, especially a lowly sophomore like me!"

"Holy crap! I can't believe you thought that of me! I'm shocked!"

His assessment was an eye-opening experience for me. I thought that I was always happy and smiling. Well, even if I wasn't always happy, I thought I was always smiling.

As I thought about it, I began to understand his perception. He only ever saw me first thing in the morning. My high school put everyone on student council (in all four grades) into the same homeroom. I was a senior and he was a sophomore. I usually arrived at school so tired from staying up late laughing with my dear friend Kristen on the phone and listening to Sexually Speaking, Dr. Ruth Westheimer's radio show. I simply could not muster a smile in our boring homeroom. That was when I realized that I had a "resting bitch face." When I wasn't actively smiling, my natural expression was a frown. Unfortunately, still is!

While it sounds counter-intuitive, a good way to boost your mood is to smile when you don't feel like it. I'm not suggesting ignoring or suppressing your feelings. Rather, I'm suggesting that smiling gets more of a positive reaction from others when you might feel depressed and need it most. So when you're feeling sad, instead of walking with your head down and shoulders slouched, lift your head and chin and smile at someone. A simple grin gets a positive reaction from others and from yourself that can shift your mood, even ever so slightly. Being beamed at is not likely to take away your sadness. But it can bring up your mood a notch.

Here's some food for thought: Did you know that a scientific study indicated that smiling is contagious? The study reported that we tend to mimic the facial expressions of others in an attempt to understand what other people are feeling, so that we may respond appropriately.[110] This response is often not even within the person's awareness or control. It's like breathing or blinking! Not only is the other person highly likely to smile back, but they probably will follow up with a response that feels good to you, such as saying hello or striking up conversation.

Several years ago, I worked with a teenage client who complained that she felt lonely walking in her high school hallways. Others were chatting and laughing, and she felt left out. I suggested that she simply try smiling at other students walking toward her and to pay attention to others' reactions.

She came in the next session and couldn't wait to tell me what happened. "Dr. Peggy! It worked!"

As we had talked about a few different issues the last session, I needed clarification. "What worked?" I asked.

"The smiling thing! Just like you said, I got smiles back! I felt visible! I felt noticed! And one kid who's in my History class even commented on my goal during my soccer game yesterday, saying it was 'epic.' And Susan said she wanted to sit with me in lunch so we could go over our notes for our Spanish class."

It was so simple, yet so powerful. She smiled at her classmates, they smiled back, and they interacted with her. She didn't feel invisible anymore.

Naturally, this works the other way, too: hanging your head and frowning are not helpful, unless your goal is for others to avoid you. Simply put, smiling at someone triggers an approach response. Frowning at someone triggers an avoidance response. So if you desire support or connection and want to elevate your mood, smile at someone. If you want to wallow in your sorrow and be left alone, then frown or be totally neutral.

Another explanation for how smiling improves mood is physiological. The act of smiling releases dopamine in your brain, which increases feelings of happiness. It also increases the release of serotonin, which is known to reduce stress and help the body relax.[111] In turn, this lowers heart rate and blood pressure.[112] And get this: it doesn't even need to be a genuine smile. So if you're feeling emotionally down in the dumps and have no reason to smile, then try one on anyway. The brain cannot distinguish the difference between a genuine smile and a made-up smile. You can actually "trick" your brain to release serotonin and dopamine—and get yourself into an improved mood![113]

Take Action

1. Look at yourself in the mirror. Do you have a "resting bitch face" like me? Is that the image you want to portray to the world? If not, practice in the mirror to discover what muscles move that frown to at least a neutral expression. This may sound funny but give it a try. Practice what it feels like to convey the smile you'd like to show the world. Other than pictures, we typically don't know what our smiles look like. When we see a picture of ourselves smiling, we don't connect it with what that feels like on our face. By consciously smiling in the mirror, we can grow familiar with how our smiles look and feel and become more aware of the face that we're presenting to the world.

2. If you are feeling sad and would like support from others, hold your head and chin up and smile at others.

3. If you are having a crummy day and need a quick mood boost, start with a smile. No matter how you're feeling, give the world the best smile that you can muster. You do not need to smile at anyone. Just form your mouth into a smile and literally trick your brain to release those neurotransmitters, resulting in an improved mood.

Chapter 26

Be Goofy

"There's power in looking silly and not caring that you do."
—Amy Poehler

Be goofy. Dance as if no one is watching. Sing as if no one is listening. As we get older, we may perceive some of the things that bring us joy as being "goofy," so we abandon them. But it is these simple daily activities or small exercises that may seem goofy that bring us happiness and joy. Think about it. It is really hard to stay in a bad mood if you do something silly. Engaging in goofy behavior is likely to result in a smile on your face, and as you learned from the previous chapter, smiling fosters happiness.

Sometimes, as we get older, we stop engaging in playful behavior because we simply do not have the time and space for it. We become consumed by our busy schedules and the stressors of life, leaving little time for play. After all, play is not considered to be a "productive" activity. Or we may stop engaging in playful behavior because we may become self-conscious and stop doing what brings us joy out of fear of judgment. We often think that others are watching our every move and evaluating us. But the reality is, nobody cares! People are wrapped up in their own lives and problems. They do not have time or energy to care. If by chance you find that anyone does care and is somehow offended by your silliness, do not take it personally! Being goofy is a wonderful way to practice not caring what others think. Paradoxically, being vulnerable and authentic in your own goofy way will actually increase your lovability.

One study found that couples who were goofy and silly together experienced more positive emotion.[114] This positive emotion in turn was associated with satisfaction in the relationship. Couples who are silly and goofy tend to feel closer to each other, have a stronger sense of security, and communicate better.[115] Contentment in our intimate relationships contributes to overall happiness and fulfillment in life.

So be your goofy self. By that, I mean do what you may have done as a child that brought you enjoyment but may seem inappropriate simply because you are an adult and you think you are expected to act a certain way. Skip if you feel like skipping. Skipping brings forth happiness. Just look at any playground. The children who are skipping are all smiling and laughing. Skipping induces the same joy in adults. Skipping can be viewed as a form of play. The National Institute for Play emphasizes the importance of play in all stages of life.

Studies demonstrate the science behind movement and emotion. The current state of the body sends messages to the brain through interoceptive and proprioceptive input, and this has an impact on emotion.[116] Therefore, through deliberate body movement, one can influence his or her emotional state. This is a basic idea used in dance/movement therapy. Body movements associated with happiness, such as skipping, have been used to purposefully boost one's mood.[117] Another study found that simply watching someone else engaged in these movements boosted mood![118]

My father taught me to love goofiness. Throughout his life, he carried that that carefree, innocent, joyful spirit that we often only see in young children. I saw it in his smile and the twinkle in his eyes. I believe this trait was very important in his work as child psychiatrist. His patients related to him and loved him.

My father skied wearing a multicolored clown wig. Showing up in this poufy wig of orange, yellow, red, green, and blue tight curls earned him smiles from strangers and often started conversations. He didn't care what others thought. The smiles that it invoked and the conversations it started made him so happy. As a teenager, I was mortified when he wore that monstrosity on his head.

My father also embarrassed me at high school. On his day off, every Wednesday, if it was not ski season, he ran around my high school track during school hours. However, he didn't run in a typical manner, or even in a straight line. He zigzagged lane to lane, performed a twirl every now and then, and often boxed the air as if he were Rocky. You can imagine how embarrassing this behavior was for me and my siblings as our classmates were out on the track for gym class.

My father passed away when he was only fifty-eight years old. Shortly after his death, when we reminisced about him, the memories of his pure goofiness helped ease our sorrow. It was hard not to smirk or chuckle when thinking about all the funny things he'd done. When I felt that my grief was going to eat me alive, I thought about him sitting at the dining room table at Thanksgiving, pulling the back of his shirt over his head so that his face stuck out of his shirt as if in a picture frame. Of course, he had corn on the cob pieces glued to his chin.

Since then, when I speak about my father, even acquaintances remember his goofiness, often with a sense of endearment and sometimes envy. I think it's that true sense of freedom that they coveted. My father sincerely did not care what others thought of him. He felt totally free, and when others were around him, they could also experience that sense of liberation.

Being child-like can make even the most mundane activities less boring and more enjoyable. So sing to the music at the grocery store. If you're shopping with a family member, play catch with the orange before putting it in the cart. If you're folding laundry with someone, put your clean underwear on your head while you fold the next shirt. I'm pretty sure it was the nightly silliness while cleaning up and playing Pictionary and Taboo after dinner during COVID-19 that got my family through each day of quarantine.

Being silly also takes the pressure off being "perfect." When you are carefree, you allow yourself to be vulnerable. Yes, there are situations where the display of your maturity and intelligence are required. But when that is not necessary, let down your guard and allow yourself to play a little. Over time, you will realize that it feels so much better to be goofy than to do everything the "right way." People also relate better to others who have a sense of humor, are authentic, and allow themselves to be vulnerable as compared to people who always have a need to be right, not make mistakes, and be perfect.[119] If you need some help with letting go of perfection, read Brené Brown's *The Gifts of Imperfection*.

Many of us would rather keep this goofy behavior for a select few, and that is fine. For me, it is my family of origin (my mother, sister, and brothers), my family (my husband, two daughters and son), and a small, select group of friends I have known since grade school.

In fact, I'm goofy on a daily basis in my household. It is the grease that keeps my family running. In between my check-ins about completing homework, requests to finish chores, and demands that dirty, wet towels go in the hamper, I am goofy. I sing at the top of my lungs with my daughters in the car. I do silly dance moves in the kitchen while making dinner. I make my fifteen-year-old son laugh by making outlandish statements, such as telling him that he could run as fast as a rocket while playing soccer if he could only fart while sprinting toward the ball.

Thankfully, my family finds this behavior amusing, and they are often silly in return. It helps maintain my patience and not scream when I have to ask for something done the fifth time! It helps to create funny memories, and it helps to ease conflict. Life is simply more fun with a bit of goofiness.

Take Action

1. The next time you perform a mundane task, spice it up with some goofiness. Pick whatever chore you like the least. If you hate mowing the lawn, try wearing a clown wig as you push the mower or sit on the tractor. Not only will you smile, but your neighbors will smile! Likewise, remember what happens when you smile? You trigger the release of feel-good neurotransmitters in your brain. Also, if anyone IS around, you're guaranteed to get a chuckle, smile, or eye roll. It can lighten any mood and make any mundane chore more tolerable.

2. Think about what fun or goofy activities you have given up since childhood. Do you avoid dancing at weddings or other events because of your concern about what others think? Stop, go out there, and do the "electric slide" or the "nae nae." What would your ten-year-old self LOVE to do that you stopped doing? Just think twice about doing a cartwheel, unless you are flexible and/or stretched those muscles. But you can certainly skip or sing "Sweet Caroline" at karaoke night. You can still be your mature-ass self while being goofy, because it's being child-like, not childish. Being goofy is a wonderful way to practice not caring. Both being goofy and not caring what others think of you will contribute to your level of happiness. You will come to know that the level of caring what others think of you is in direct proportion to your sense of freedom. Period.

Gratitude

Chapter 27

Develop a Gratitude Mindset

"Gratitude unlocks the fullness of life."
–Melody Beattie

Practicing gratitude has numerous benefits. Gratitude is a state of being thankful. I incorporate methods of expressing appreciation and thankfulness into just about every workshop I deliver related to mental health. Why? Because it is probably the easiest and most enjoyable way to elevate mood. It does not just help for the moment; when practiced regularly, it provides long-term positive effects. Practicing gratitude has psychological benefits of expanding happiness[120] and boosting resilience,[121], physical benefits of improving sleep[122] and increasing energy[123], social benefits of offering support to others[124] and helping marriages,[125] and career benefits of motivating employees.[126]

I have been delivering presentations on Gratitude for about six years and now. I have been a speaker at World Gratitude Summit with Jack Canfield and Hal Elrod, and I have an eight-week online Course in Gratitude available at https://drpeggydelong.thinkific.com/courses/a-course-in-gratitude. I am always looking for more inspirational information on gratitude practices and research demonstrating the brain science and effectiveness of practicing gratitude. I was delighted to come across this article that summarized thirty-one ways that practicing gratitude positive impacts our lives. What's more, the piece provides a link to the research behind each claim.

Here are the thirty-one benefits as listed in the article:[127]

- Fosters happiness.
- Enhances likability.
- Strengthens physical health.
- Boosts careers.
- Helps us to have less envy and jealousy.
- Deepens positive emotions.
- Develops our personality.
- Supports physiological functioning.
- Increases longevity
- Makes us more likely to exercise.
- Fuels resilience.
- Creates a positive emotion
- Improves marriages.
- Makes us more attractive.
- Helps make friends.
- Facilitates networking.
- Decreases materialism.
- Encourages spiritualism.
- Reduces self-centeredness.
- Increases self-esteem.
- Enhances decision-making.
- Improves physical health by decreasing stress.
- Creates happier memories.
- Fosters relaxation.
- Develops a friendlier appearance.

- Deepens relationships.
- Increases goal attainment.
- Amplifies productivity.
- Improves sleep.
- Fosters optimism.
- Boosts energy levels.

It's pretty amazing that just doing one thing, practicing gratitude, can achieve all those results! But how do you get started? What does it mean to "practice gratitude?" Here are some basic exercises to do every day. They take very little time are very easy to do. Yet when done on a regular basis, these small actions can profoundly and positively impact not just your day, but your overall life experience.

Say "thank you" before getting out of bed.

When we say the two words "thank you", we are priming our brains to be more positive. This is because our whole lives, these words have been associated with positivity. We thank people for nice, positive things, not for crummy, negative things! Keep in mind when you say these two words, you do not even need to be thinking about what you are thankful for. Just focus on saying a heartfelt "thank you". Your brain will do the rest! Your brain receives a dose of "feel-good" neurotransmitters, and you are setting the stage for your brain to notice all that is good around you. You are beginning your day in the most positive way and also heightening your level of awareness of all the good things that happen throughout the day.

Make a conscious decision to focus on gratitude throughout the day.

When we set our intention, we are activating a part of our brain called the Reticular Activating System. This is the part of the brain that works as a filtering system and sorts through all of the millions of pieces of data that bombard our senses every day. Setting our intention to focus on gratitude magnifies our ability to notice and celebrate the good things and pay less attention to the negative things. Or better yet, you may not even notice them at all! Setting our intention helps the Reticular Activating System do its job. Focusing on gratitude does not change the world, but it transforms the way we see the world. We are better able to see the wonderful things, big and small, and pay less attention to or not even notice the negative things.

Do the Hand Exercise (a favorite).

Look at your hand and use your fingers to foster positive thoughts and gratitude. Look at your thumb and think of one thing that you have done that you are proud of. Check out your pointer and point to one beautiful thing in nature, or in the room. Next is your middle finger. Instead of cursing someone by giving "it" to them, think of a time that you have blessed someone's life. Then look at your ring finger and think about when you have felt loved by someone, or when you have expressed love. Finally, glance at your pinky, and think of one small thing for which you are grateful.[128]

In my workshop and online Course in Gratitude, I share exercises in gratitude to incorporate into our lives that are more involved in time and energy than the suggestions above that simply involve the mind. Some take a few moments; others are planned and take more time. Some involve thinking, while others require action. Don't try to do them all. Just pick what resonates with you. The idea is to do what feels good, not to add one more thing to your to-do list. Some have their own chapter in this book, but I am mentioning them briefly in this section, as they are related to gratitude.

Create a gratitude journal.

Spend two to three minutes a day thinking about new things you are grateful for. This is the easiest and quickest way to boost your mood. Try it for a month.

Make sure that the list is different every day. Be specific. For example, instead of writing that you are grateful for your spouse, write something that your spouse does for you for which you are grateful. This is powerful and effective because you are training your brain to see the world differently, to look for the positive. This is a quick way of learning and practicing optimism.

The research demonstrates that you can maximize the benefits of using a gratitude journal if you: 1) write something different every day, and 2) be specific.[129] Using this research, I created a gratitude journal with thirty different writing prompts. The writing prompts then repeat twelve times to make a year-long gratitude journal. You can find out more information about this journal on my website: www. peggysmidnightcreations.com/ product/gratitude-journal/

Keep it simple. You are more likely to follow through if you keep it to two to three minutes, and you write about two things. It does not need to be fancy. Keep your ideas on your phone, in a spiral notebook, or on a pad of paper. As an added bonus, not only do we feel better in the moment, but being grateful actually brings more goodness into our lives.

Try team gratitude.

Pick a friend, family member, or acquaintance who is willing to make a commitment to share thoughts of gratitude with you for a specific amount of time, such as every day for one week. When the time is over, find a new person. Text or email your thoughts to each other by the end of the day. Having another person's perspective and ideas can open your mind to things to be grateful for that you may have overlooked. This exercise also helps keep you accountable. Also, connecting with another person every day feeds your human need to be social.

Ask yourself and others gratitude-inspired questions.

At the end of the day, ask yourself or someone else some thought-provoking gratitude questions. One option is to write these down on slips on paper, put them in a jar, and pick one or two a night. You could do this at bedtime with a child or during family dinner conversation.

For example, "What made me laugh today?" "What made my life easier today?" "What five or ten minutes would I love to do over again?" "Who or what touched me emotionally today?" "What was the best thing that happened to me or someone I care about?"

Do without.

For a week (or for a day if a week is too much), go without something. We often can take for granted the simple aspects of daily living in the twenty-first century. When we try to go without something we are used to having, we begin to appreciate and be more grateful for it. This became clearly evident during COVID-19 when so many simple pleasures of daily living were not possible. But we don't need a pandemic to appreciate these things. Try going without television, take-out food, or restaurant meals for a month. Or don't buy something, such as a cup of coffee or ice cream, when you feel like it.

You can also imagine doing without something, such as the ability to see, hear, or walk, or anything that provides you with comfort. Visualize life without it, and then imagine the gratitude when getting it back.

Recall a difficult situation.

Sometimes we forget to appreciate how far we've come. Think about a bad or difficult situation that you overcame. Remember how difficult it was and think about how far you have come. Be grateful for your progress and the positive qualities you possess that helped you get there (courage, motivation, determination, strength).

Be grateful for a special person.

Think about someone you are grateful for. Imagine something specific that this person did or does for you. Picture that person in your mind and all his or her positive qualities. Consider what that person has taught you, done for you, and the positive impact on your life.

Use uncomfortable or painful emotions as a trigger to practice gratitude.

This exercise can take great effort, particularly in difficult situations. However, it is possible to find one thing to be grateful for, even in bad times. Some examples: While waiting in a long line at a store, you can be grateful that you were able to find and buy what you wanted. If you are stuck in traffic due to an accident, you can be grateful that you are not involved in it. If an appointment is canceled, you can be grateful for the unexpected free time. During these trying times, think to yourself, "What can this teach me?" "What can I learn from this situation?" "How can I grow from this?" "What small good thing can I find in this?"

Doing this process is how I stumbled on the power of gratitude. I didn't know what I was doing at the time. All I knew was that it helped me through one of the most painful times in my life.

During the last forty-two days of my fiancé's life while he was in the hospital, I never knew what condition he was going to be in, whether he would be able to talk or look at me, or which nurses and doctors would be working. But one thing was consistent: my cup of hazelnut coffee. The smell seemed to permeate his hospital room and make it less sterile. I was comforted by the warmth from the cup.

Hazelnut coffee gave me simple pleasure through its taste, but even more so, its predictable availability in a very anxiety-provoking, unpredictable time. My fiancé knew how much that cup of coffee meant to me; he encouraged me to stretch my legs and go to the cafeteria to get it or to ask someone to get it for me when he didn't want me to leave his side. We were both grateful for the simple pleasure of that predictable hazelnut coffee. It kept me company when I was feeling alone and scared. Enjoying and feeling grateful for that hazelnut coffee are what got me through those days. Sitting next to him while he slept and holding his hand with my left hand while writing in my journal with my right hand. The simple joy of walking with him around the halls of his oncology floor when he felt well enough to get out of bed. He wore his white terry cloth robe and slippers that scraped across the hard floor and waved to everyone with an open hospital room door. It is possible to find gratitude in awful situations. Sometimes, it's the only thing you can do to survive. I share this with you to demonstrate that even when you are living a nightmare, it is possible to be grateful for one thing. When you are able to do so, you will feel better.

Start the day with mindful gratitude.

An easy way to incorporate gratitude is to focus on it when doing routine morning tasks. While eating breakfast, pay attention to the way the food tastes. If you are drinking a warm beverage, cup your hands around the mug and feel the warmth. Take in the smell of what you are eating and drinking. Look out the window and appreciate what you see, and that you have eyes to see it.

Sit in the Gratitude Chair.

This exercise works with a group of people that meets regularly. It could be a family dinner, a coffee group, or students at a lunch table. When you are together, have one person sit in the Gratitude Chair. Each person makes a comment of gratitude for the person in the designated seat. If you have many people in your group and you meet often, you could do this more than once a week. If it is a large group, pick one person to be in charge of tracking who has had a turn to sit in the Gratitude Chair so that everyone has a chance to hear the wonderful things that people have to say about them.

Send a thank-you note.

Who is one person who has had a positive impact on your life? Using a store-bought, hand-made, or computer-generated one, write and send a thank-you note. It could be for a single action or an ongoing way this person influences you in a positive way. It could be someone from your past, or someone who continues to have a positive presence in your life.

Surprise the people you know and send one out every week or month. Or really take this on and send a thank-you note every day, for acts big and small, as part of your daily routine. Not only will this make the recipient happy but practicing this kind of gratitude will continually lift your spirits by remembering something special that was done for you. It also increases social connectedness, which tends to make us happier. One study found that college students who received counseling who also wrote one thank you note a week for three weeks reported significantly better mental health functioning four weeks later as compared to a group that received counseling alone.[130]

John Kralik wrote a thank-you note every day, and it changed his life. He wrote about it in his book, *365 Thank Yous: The Year a Simple Act of Gratitude Changed My Life*. Purchase the book or audible, and you are guaranteed to be inspired.

Appreciate sensory experiences.

Focus on the senses that we so often take for granted. Note the taste and texture of what you are eating and be thankful for it. When listening to music, close your eyes and focus on the talent of the musician, the combinations and varieties of sounds. Be grateful for your ability to hear them with your ears. When outside, take in the aroma of nature and appreciate the different scents. Throughout the day, pay attention to the different textures that your hands touch and be grateful for your ability to feel.

Purchase or make a gratitude bracelet.

Buy or make a multicolored beaded bracelet. Each color can represent something you are grateful for. For example, red can represent your gratitude for the love in your family, green can stand for the money you have, pink can symbolize your friendships. When you wear the bracelet, look at and touch each bead, calling to mind what it represents. The bracelet can also consist of symbolic charms.

Two years ago, I combined my passion for helping people improve their mental health with my zeal for making jewelry by creating the Gratitude Bracelet. The bracelet is simple in design and powerful in impact. It is made of one gemstone and one center bead of the person's choosing. When your eye is drawn to the center metal bead, it is a reminder to stop and take a brief moment in gratitude. It is a wearable, visual reminder to pause and think of one person, situation, thing, or experience for which you are grateful. A friend best referred to it as a "pep talk on my wrist." You can customize and purchase your own from my website: www.drpeggydelong.com.

Engage in random acts of kindness.

One way to express gratitude for what you have is by giving to others. Pay for the person in line behind you at the coffee shop. Leave an inspirational note on a stranger's windshield. Compliment someone while you are running errands.

Once while I was out grocery shopping, there was a young mother with two children checking out a full cart of groceries. After she had all of the items through the scanner and bagged in her cart, she realized that she forgot her wallet with her credit card. She found some cash in her pocket, but it was not enough to cover all of the groceries. The person behind her offered to pay the balance. The woman with children asked to take down her name and address so that she could mail her a check. The generous older woman declined and told her to simply pay it forward. Sometimes situations like this arise which give us the opportunity to randomly bestow kindness upon a stranger.

Plan acts of kindness.

This process involves more time, organization, and planning, but is so rewarding. Plan an activity or outing for others. Giving to others makes us more grateful for what we have, especially when we feel that we do not have much to give. The possibilities are endless:

- Give to the food pantry.
- Volunteer at a soup kitchen.
- Donate gently used toys and clothes.
- Organize a toy or food drive.
- Sing at a senior center or for veterans.
- Make cards for soldiers.
- Make placemats for community meal delivery.

Say thank you out loud.

Every time something is done for you, say "thank you" out loud. Thank the person who held the door open for you; thank the grocery cashier who bagged your items. You can make an even greater positive impact by adding a few words to your thank-you message. When appropriate, be specific. For example, when someone holds the door open for you, instead of just saying, "thank you," which we do by habit, say, "Thank you for holding the door for me. That was so kind of you." It feels even better to the recipient because it increases the level of social interaction, something most of us need.

Share gratitude with others.

Involve other people in the gratitude experience. For instance, at dinner time say grace before eating. Or go around the table and each person says one or two things for which they are grateful (even if it's not Thanksgiving). Make a gratitude jar and fill it with short, handwritten notes of what each person is grateful for, and then review them together once a week, or at Thanksgiving or another special occasion. As you go about our day, take photos representing gratitude and share them daily or at a once-a-week, picture-sharing meal.

Walk with gratitude.

While out for a walk or running errands, make a conscious effort to pay attention to the positive information coming through your senses, and be grateful for them. Do you smell flowers, grass, leaves, or the aroma from a restaurant or someone's kitchen? Do you see a beautiful yard, pet, butterfly, or storefront? In particular, do this in areas that are familiar to you; be grateful for what you may have missed before, simply because it is routine.

Be grateful during ordinary days.

Some days are filled with routine activities and responsibilities. Even in these ordinary times, we can be grateful. For example, when doing laundry, be thankful for the washing machine and that we have people we love in our lives whose clothes we wash. Or just be grateful that it is "ordinary," because that also means we aren't experiencing a crisis. Ordinary days can feel extraordinary when we celebrate them and express gratitude for their simplicity.

When I mentioned this exercise during my gratitude presentations, I always got the impression that this was the audience's least favorite. They didn't seem to connect to the idea, understand it, or feel like it was a worthwhile endeavor. Now, since COVID-19, people can appreciate when I talk about being grateful for an ordinary day. Grateful for the ability to leave our homes and gather with friends. Grateful for coffee shops and restaurants. Grateful for beaches, parks, and hair salons. Gratitude for the simple and the ordinary becomes more special when we have been deprived of these simple pleasures.

Take Action

1. Make a conscious decision to incorporate gratitude into everyday living. Do one simple gratitude activity every day.

2. Engage in one gratitude activity every week that involves more time, energy, and/or planning.

3. Every night before you go to bed, think of one thing you are grateful for.

4. To help you incorporate gratitude into your life immediately, I have summarized my most requested presentation, "Five Daily Exercises in Gratitude in Less Than Five Minutes a Day" into a page that you can download from my website. These activities will take you from your first waking moment of the day to the minute you put your head on your pillow to go to bed, helping you to have your best day and your best lift possible. https://drpeggydelong.com/5-daily-gratitude-exercises-in-less-than-5-minutes-to-change-your-life/

5. In my monthly membership community, Feeling Good with Dr. Peggy, the month of June was dedicated to practicing gratitude. There, you will find 30 different ways to practice gratitude, along with videos, additional resources, and downloadable worksheets. https://drpeggydelong.thinkific.com/courses/feeling-good-with-dr-peggy

Chapter 28

Say Thank You

"Two simple words that can take you far in life: 'Thank you.'
Don't underestimate their power."
–Jaclyn McNeil

How many times a day do you silently think about something that someone has done for you? It could have been this morning, yesterday, or twenty years ago. It could have been something small, such as picking up your child when you were stuck in traffic, or huge, such as having a successful surgery. Who has had a positive impact on your life?

We all have these fleeting thoughts during the day. Sometimes they are so quick that we don't notice them. Or these instances happen regularly, or we expect them, so we take them for granted.

Thinking about that person and what he/she has done for you is one way to elevate your mood. Take it a step further and spend time writing a thank-you note. Or go out of your way to thank someone in person. As creatures who need social interaction, feeling connected to others is important for our mental health. Thanking someone for what that they did for you is one way to foster that connection. Besides, you never know where that may lead. The interaction may provide you with the opportunity to rekindle a relationship that was important to you during a previous time in your life.

Expressing appreciation is one of the quickest and easiest way to improve a relationship, even for things that are expected. Yes, your son or partner is supposed to take out the trash. So when they do, and you thank them for it, it leaves them with a positive feeling toward themselves, as well as toward you. Depending on your child's age, you may be expected to make dinner. How great does it feel when an eight-year-old thanks you for the meal?

In fact, this phenomenon is supported by research. Nathaniel Lambert found that saying thank you and expressing gratitude strengthened relationships.[131] More specifically, the person who expressed the gratitude perceived the relationship to be stronger. This is a great finding, because it suggests that you experience the direct benefit of your own kindness. What's more, adding the impact of their action on you provides the cherry on top: "Thank you for making dinner. When I come home from work and you have dinner made, it makes me feel so special." "Thank you for cleaning the bathroom. It means a lot to me that you take the time to do that." "Thank you for buying my favorite dessert. It makes me feel loved when you do these things for me."

Brighten someone's day by reaching out to a person from your past who has had an impact on you. Notice how you feel when you make the call or send the email. That elevation in mood is a sweet result. Even if the shift is small, it may be just what you need to get out of a bad mood or a downward spiral. You never know what can happen.

For instance, in 2015, I was in Vermont with my daughter for a late-season ski trip. It dawned on me that it was exactly twenty-five years to the day since my knee surgery that took place while I was a student at the University of Vermont. Since I was away with my sweet daughter doing something I love to do, I was overcome with gratitude that my procedure was everything the surgeon promised. I remember telling him, "I don't want the surgery if I can't ski the way I want to." He said I would.

So I looked him up online, and sure enough, he was listed as professor emeritus with the school. I googled his name and discovered that he had authored hundreds of articles about knee surgery. I finally found an email for him, so I wrote this letter to him:

Hello Dr. Johnson,

As I went to bed last night, it dawned on me that it was exactly twenty-five years to the day that you performed ACL reconstruction on my knee on 4/13/90! I fell skiing at Sugarbush on 3/30/90 and had a pretty bad ACL tear. I was a senior at UVM, and I graduated on crutches! After a year of rehab, I have consistently skied 40+ days every year. I just enjoyed my last day of the season on the slopes at Killington. I still ski bumps, telemark ski, mountain bike, and even ran a half-marathon, all without pain. I'd never even know that I had surgery!

So twenty-five years later, I want to thank you for the excellent work on my knee. I am so grateful that I have been able to maintain the lifestyle that is so important to me all these years, and without pain, discomfort, or scaling back!

Peggy Doherty DeLong, UVM '90"

To my surprise and delight, he wrote me back:

Dear Peggy,

Thanks for the twenty-five-year follow-up report and your kind words. It is always fun to hear about good outcomes. Hope you have many more years of skiing and no problems with your knee in the future.

Thanks again,

Robert Johnson

Take Action

1. As you go about your day, notice what others do for you. Pay attention to the kind things people say or do to lift your spirits or make your life easier. As thoughts of someone doing something kind for you come up, hold that person in your mind. Whether it is in the past or present, think about their giving actions. Say thank you in the moment, or make a point to call or send a thank-you note.

2. Be proactive and purchase or make thank-you notes. I can't tell you how many times I've wanted to send someone a note but didn't have any handy. So always keep a stash at home.

3. Notice. Notice how YOU feel when you thank someone and celebrate that feeling.

4. Go above and beyond. This person did something special for you. Now you have the opportunity to make that person feel appreciated through your simple act of saying thanks.

5. Before you go to bed tonight, write one simple thank-you note. Include what that person did for you, why it was special, and how it made you feel.

Chapter 29

Practice Self-Care

"All of us can improve the quality of our lives
if we practice the art of self-care and train our minds
to think thoughts that make us feel good."
–Louise Hay

You are a unique, separate person. You are you! Yes, you are your husband's partner, or your mother's son, or your daughter's mother, or your father's son. But don't lose sight of who you are in these relationships. Sometimes when we are so involved in a relationship or a caregiving role, we can lose sight of ourselves. It is not selfish to engage in self-care. It is necessary. In fact, your life depends upon it.

I thought that this chapter includes other ideas that are mentioned in other chapters, and that it would be redundant. Then I thought that self-care definitely deserves its own chapter. But this chapter is more about mindset. Think of it as developing a mindset of self-care, in order to engage in all of the other suggestions in this book. The importance of self-care became highlighted during COVID-19. Every commercial on television, every good friend, every health professional was talking about the importance of self-care during this difficult life experience.

I thought I was pretty good at self-care until I began working on this chapter and realized that I was not doing many of my own suggestions.

I almost did not include this chapter because I thought, "How can I talk about self-care when I am not good at it? I'd be a hypocrite suggesting these things when I am not doing them myself!" Then I realized that it's not necessary for me to have mastered something in order to help others with it. In fact, my struggles with this are relatable and may be what helps others.

So I convinced myself to begin writing this chapter. After all, I am not a master at all of my other ideas. They are simply suggestions that work for me, and things I strive for, not master.

As I began writing, I at least felt good that this particular night I was doing a pretty good job of self-care. I took the evening off from responsibilities to do what fuels my soul—kayaking on my favorite lake in the Pocono Mountains of Pennsylvania, and watching the sun set from the middle of the lake. This was followed by another activity that fuels my soul—writing, specifically, this chapter. My intention was to kayak, hammer out a chapter or two at our Pocono vacation home without distraction, and then come home to my family in the morning.

Then, an unexpected crisis happened. I woke up at 3:00 AM with terrible chest pain. It was so intense that I sat straight up in bed. I was still groggy, and I thought it must be heartburn. So I did some deep breathing to try to get through the pain, and I stood up to head toward the bathroom to get some Tums.

And the pain increased.

It was so intense, I thought, "This is not heartburn. I am having a heart attack. This is what happens to women. They think they have heartburn, but they are really having a heart attack." And I was by myself.

My father died at fifty-eight from a sudden heart attack in 1994. So it has always been a fear that it can happen to me too, especially now that I am fifty-two.

So I convinced myself that I was having a heart attack. Then the whooshing sound in my ears began, and my vision became blurry. I thought, "This is it. I am dying. My poor husband and children." I reached for my phone and called 911.

I managed to say, "I think I'm having a heart attack," before I passed out. I woke up on the floor. I had no idea how much time had passed, and I had no idea what was happening to me. I picked up the phone laying on the floor next to me, and I remembered that I had dialed 911. I said, "Hello? Hello? Hello? Hello? Hello?" But no one responded. I felt like I was in a dream. Or a nightmare. No one was on the other end of the call. Then I realized that the call had been dropped. I managed to call back. The 911 dispatcher said to me in an angry voice, "Why did you hang up on me?" I replied, "I didn't hang up on you. I passed out." He commented that it sounded like I was having trouble breathing, and all I said was. "Send someone fast!"

About five minutes later, someone from security from my gated community arrived at my door. He asked, "You called for an ambulance for your head?" I said, "No, not my head. Chest pain. I had chest pain and thought I was having a heart attack, and then I passed out."

He replied, "Well, then you must have hit your head when you passed out. You are bleeding. You have a big gash on your forehead."

I had no idea. I must have been in a state of shock. I did not even feel it. I felt no pain on my head. Mysteriously, I had no more pain in my chest, either. I touched my eyebrow, which appeared to have a big clump of blood on it. Thankfully, my eyebrow caught the trickling blood, so it was not running down my face. Quickly, I took my finger away. I did not want to feel it, and I certainly did not want to see it.

While I was still in this groggy state, the ambulance arrived and took me to the local hospital. I managed to call my husband at 3:30 AM to ask him to meet me there. He had to wake up our three teens and tell them what was going on, so that they would not wake up in the morning and wonder where he was.

I remained in the hospital all weekend. They ran every test possible to assess my heart and head. I passed every test with flying colors. Thank God nothing was wrong with my heart. It remains a mystery what the heck happened. I still do not have an answer regarding what the chest pain was all about and why it woke me up. But it was unlike any pain I had ever experienced before. I believe I have an explanation for passing out, though. Vasovagal syncope—fight or flight. I believe that I passed out from pure fear.

Although I was given a clean bill of health, the experience was a huge eye-opener for me. I thought all weekend while in the hospital – "What can I do to take better care of myself?" I decided to keep it simple, and I am sharing those basic ideas with you. As you know, I am no expert at these, so I encourage you to do further reading in the areas where you think you need some work.

Eat well.

OK, I'm starting with this one, because this is the most difficult for me. I have been reading a lot of interesting stuff lately about how what's in our gut is related to mental health. This is a whole book in itself and is not an area of my expertise, so I will not attempt to write about it. However, it is essential for self-care, so I am including it in this chapter and providing some resources.

A few suggestions regarding gut and mental health:

The Mind-Gut Connection: How the Hidden Conversation within our Bodies Impacts Our Mood, Our Choices, and Our Overall Health by Emeran Mayer

The Gut-Brain Connection: Altering Your Diet to Improve Your Emotional Health by Cullen Hardy

Gut Psychology: The Most Comprehensive and Empirically Researched Dietary Program for Mental Health by Dr. Nicole Cain

Also, some people swear by **plant-based eating**. Here are a few suggestions for further reading if you would like to take that approach.

Forks Over Knives: The Plant-Based Way to Health by Gene Stone

The Forks Over Knives Plan: How to Transition to the Life-Saving, Whole-Food, Plant-Based Diet by Alona Pulde MD and Matthew Lederman MD.

And for some, **emotional eating** is what gets in the way of health. Here are some suggestions if you feel that you need to address the relationship between your emotions and food.

Intuitive Eating: A Revolutionary Program that Works by Evelyn Tribole MD and Elyse Resch MS, RD, FADA

Never Binge Again: Reprogram Yourself to Think Like a Permanently Thin Person by Glenn Livingston, MD

Get Adequate Sleep.

Disruptions in sleep affect the brain, and this in turn affects emotional regulation and impairs thinking. This often exacerbates any current problems. In other words, a person with anxiety may experience more anxiety when sleep deprived. A person with depressed mood may feel more depressed with lack of sleep. A person with symptoms of attention deficit disorder may experience increased difficulties concentrating and attending with lack of sleep.[132]

In my own practice, many of my clients coming to me for help with emotional issues are also experiencing problems related to sleep. For some, this can be related to racing thoughts at bedtime when they are trying to fall asleep or when they wake up in the middle of the night. You can find an article I wrote, "Coping with Racing Thoughts or Worries" on my website. https://drpeggydelong.com/coping-with-racing-thoughts-at-bedtime/

For further reading and help with sleep:

Sleep Soundly Every Night, Feel Fantastic Every Day: A Doctor's Guide to Solving Your Sleep Problems by Robert Rosenberg, DO, FCCP

Maintain hydration.

Simply drinking water has been associated with decreased symptoms of depression and anxiety.[133] Drinking water is probably the easiest thing you can do to boost your mental health.

And some other important tips for self-care—Exercise, Accept/Ask for Help. Speak Your Truth, spend time with friends (Connect with People), and hobbies/finding joy (Do What Makes Your Soul Happy). All of these items are vital self-care activities and have their own chapters in this book.

Chapter 30

Do What Makes Your Soul Happy

*"If you feel like there's something out there
that you're supposed to be doing, if you have a passion for it,
then stop wishing and just do it."*
—Wanda Sykes

One simple way to live a more fulfilling life is to do what brings you joy. This helps combat depression and anxiety and makes stressful situations and life crises more bearable.

I've always been drawn to positive psychology, even before I knew it had a name. I was raised by a child psychiatrist who enjoyed reading about and practicing methods of living a fulfilling life, to help his patients, and to help himself. My father knew how to live. When I think back on his life, what resonates with me is that my father always took time out to fuel his soul and do what made him happy. He did so while busy with a thriving private practice, and while being an active and loving father to four children. I never saw his pursuit of enjoyment as selfish. That is a priceless gift that he taught me through his behavior. He sought joy, he was joyful, and he was a joy to be around.

Being able to find joy in everyday living is now something that I emphasize with my clients. As I am putting the finishing touches on some mental health/positive psychology workshops, I repeatedly find myself stressing the importance of discovering joy, even in the darkness and corners when it cannot easily be found.

I have worked with busy mothers and teenagers in my private practice for eighteen years, and I have noticed some resistance to finding joy. Excuses such as, "I'm too busy," "I have too much homework," "There's no time to do what I really love," "I don't even know what brings me joy," and "That's selfish. I've got kids who need me."

I am editing this chapter in the midst of COVID19. It has become even more clear that joy helps us get through difficult times. The problem is that during times of crisis, grief, or tragedy, many people feel that they do not deserve to experience joy. They think it's selfish, hedonistic, or inappropriate. However, it is during these times that we need joy the most. We cannot control what's going on in the world, but we can influence our own lives in a positive way by cultivating joy. For example, I cannot change the fact we cannot have a graduation party for my high school graduate due to COVID19, but I can incorporate joy into daily family life through simple activities, such as playing Pictionary after dinner. The game is guaranteed to bring laughter in my family. We often laugh uncontrollably at my awful drawings and how my daughters are able to guess each other's pictures with a single stroke. My husband and I don't stand a chance when we're paired against this dynamic duo!

When it comes to creating your own joy, I'm here to tell you, "Get out of your own way!" First of all, it is not selfish. Doing what brings you joy or makes your soul happy actually makes you the best version of yourself. It makes your interactions with all of those around you more loving and pleasant. It makes you a better friend, mother, wife, etc. Doing what brings you enjoyment elevates mood, and that elevated mood in turn affects your behavior and interactions with others. Think of it as your positive mood being contagious, because science demonstrates that it is! So if you still are struggling with the idea that doing what you love is selfish, think of it as one way that you can give to others by "contaminating" them with your better mood, and giving them your best self.

It is also important to remember that there is only one person in charge of your life, of your happiness, and that is you! You have choices, and you can choose to engage in activities that bring you joy and fulfillment. No one else can do that for you. It is up to you to make the time for it.

And if improving your emotional health is not a sufficient reason for you to engage in doing what makes your soul happy, remember that this way of life also benefits your physical health. Engaging in enjoyable activities reduces stress, and we all know that reduced stress means reduced physical illness.

In my work, I frequently hear people say that they are too "busy" with school, work, and/or parenthood to pursue joy. One way to address this is to make an appointment with yourself. Yes, that's right. Make an appointment with yourself. Put it in Google Calendar or write in on the paper calendar. And then keep this appointment. Block out the time and write "me time." Make a weekly appointment with yourself to do what makes your soul happy. Block out a half day if you can. Paradoxically, the "busy" person who takes time out for joy is more energized and productive.

It is also important for "busy" people to find enjoyment every day. This need not involve a lot of time, but it is important to do. I look back to the "busiest" year of my life when I was in graduate school. I woke up at 5:45 AM, drove an hour to work and got there by 8:00 AM. I worked at a hospital with children with cancer from 8:00 AM until 3:00 PM. Then I had another hour of driving and taking the train to take two classes in New York City. One at 4:00-6:40, and the other. 7:00-9:40. Then I had about a ninety-minute commute home. I was a broke student, and I could not afford to eat out. So once I got home, I made and packed my breakfast, lunch, and dinner for the next day. By then it was midnight. And then I did it all over again, and again, and again. But during the twenty minutes I had free from 6:40-7:00, I always did something I enjoyed.

I ate dinner with a classmate. I walked toward South Street Seaport. I listened to music. Also, before I went to bed, I always made sure that I had at least five minutes of doing something I enjoyed, such as reading, and spending time with my husband. I simply could not have gotten through that time without doing something that brought me pure joy every day. Even though the amount of time was quite short, it gave me something to look forward to. It was the gift that I gave myself every single day. So if you are a busy student/mother/father/worker/business owner, give yourself the gift of at least five minutes of joy before going to bed.

There will also be times that a life crisis is so heavy and sad that it paralyzes you. Even during these times, it is possible to find joy. During my fiancé's last hospital stay as he battled cancer, friends and family sent him many cards that we posted all over the walls of his room. One day, during a quiet day with just my father and me in the room with him, he looked at his cards. Then looked at me and said, "There is so much love in this room." He then looked at my father and said, "I love your daughter." Even when he knew that his death was imminent, he was able to find joy. Because he felt love.

With this experience I learned the valuable lesson that when we're having difficulty finding joy on our darkest day, we can look for love. What love can you find around you? If you are suffering due to difficulty in an important relationship, who is loving you and supporting you through it? And don't forget to include yourself.

Finding joy and doing what makes your soul happy need not be extravagant. It can be a simple enjoyment. In fact, during a time of crisis, simple may be better.

This became clear for many families during COVID-19. During an extremely difficult time of confinement to our homes, we had no choice but to find joy in very simple things. One of the simple ways that I brought joy to our dinner table was to use the good china that had previously only been used for when we had guests at Thanksgiving every year.

Take Action

1. Become aware of and attack the thoughts, or excuses, that are interfering with your ability to do what makes your soul happy. "I'm too busy," "My kids come first," "That's selfish," "I don't deserve it." Take out a piece of paper. On the left-hand side, write down the negative thought that prevents you from seeking or experiencing joy. On the right-hand side, write the statement with a positive slant. For example, "That's selfish" becomes, "I serve my family and friends better when I am joyful." Similarly, "I'm too busy" becomes, "I schedule time for what's important to me. Experiencing joy is crucial to my well-being."

2. If you find yourself unsure of what brings you joy, this is a sign that you need more joy in your life! You may need to start by spending time discovering what brings you joy. Try out new activities. Do something that you used to do that brought you joy in the past.

3. Practice positive affirmations around doing what makes your soul happy: "Doing what makes my soul happy helps me to be my best self," "My elevated mood helps to elevate the mood of those around me," "Doing what makes me happy improves my physical health."

4. Make a weekly appointment with yourself and KEEP it. You are in charge of your life. It is up to you to make the time for enjoyment.

5. Find something that you can do every day for at least five minutes that you can engage in on your busiest of days.

6. Make lists and make appointments with yourself. In my membership community, Feeling Good with Dr. Peggy, I encourage members to make three lists. The first list consists of activities that you enjoy that take five to ten minutes. Make an appointment with yourself to do something from this list every day. Make another list of activities that

take thirty to sixty minutes. Make an appointment with yourself to do these activities three to five times a week. Make a third list of activities that take a half day or full day. Schedule time on your calendar to do these activities every week or every other week.

7. Shift your thinking to find gratitude during busy days.

8. It is important during life crises to engage in simple acts that bring comfort. Read. Laugh with a loved one. Listen to music. Write. Take a bath. Drink hazelnut coffee.

9. When life feels too heavy or sad to do anything joyful, look for love. For example, if you are going through a painful time of your life, ask yourself, "Who is showing me love?" or ask, "Who do I love?" When you find love, you will experience joy. If you cannot readily find it, create it. Reach out to someone and communicate your love, or refer to a suggestion in the chapter, "Give to Others." When you create your own love or act of love, you will experience joy.

Chapter 31

Maintain Perspective

"Positive people are able to maintain a broader perspective and see the big picture which helps them identify solutions whereas negative people maintain a narrower perspective and tend to focus on problems."
–Barbara Fredrickson

Throughout our days, we can become stressed or upset about so many different things! If something is bothering you, ask yourself, "Does this really matter?" and "At the end of the day, does this really have an impact on my life or the lives of the ones I love?" You will be able to live a happier life if you are able to maintain a broad outlook and focus on solutions while simultaneously setting aside the thoughts, problems, and worries that really do not matter at the end of the day.[134]

If you are struggling with a problem, contemplate this—"Does this really matter in my life?" Play it out. How does it matter? Why does it matter? Challenge yourself. Take it to the worst-case scenario. Think about, "Yes, it matters because… And then that would mean…. And then this would happen…" When you do this and think about what the real fear is, it helps you to realize that the fear is fabricated. It is something created in your head. Then you may discover that it really does not matter. Then choose to label the fear for what it is and choose to let it go!

Most often, when we ask ourselves, "Does this really matter?" the answer will be no. I'm not talking about serious relationship problems or a health crisis. I'm talking about ruminating about something you said or worrying about what someone thinks of you. The stuff that really does not matter. Rumination means repeatedly and continuously thinking about the past. Most often when we ruminate, it is in relation to negative experiences. It is important to recognize when we are ruminating and to make efforts to stop, as rumination has been linked with depression and anxiety.[135] If the answer is that it does matter, then you know that it is something that deserves your energy and attention. Then you can make a plan to do something about it. Write down your goal and steps or solutions to achieve it. Having a plan can help you to feel better.

Sometimes our life challenges teach us to keep things in perspective by reminding us what really does matter. Most of us have experienced a crisis that is so big that all of the smaller problems become totally insignificant or completely off our radar. It is during these times that we learn what is truly important.

Being able to see "the big picture" helps to keep things in perspective and let go of the things that do not matter, appreciate the good things that do matter, and be better able to find solutions to the problems that do matter. The beauty of keeping things in perspective is the happiness that follows. When we free ourselves of concerns and worries about things that really do not impact our lives, it allows us to be more present in our lives, and it creates space for more positivity.

Unfortunately, this is a lesson that often comes in the midst of a crisis. When you are consumed with a job loss, loss of a relationship, illness diagnosis, or death of a loved one, you simply do not have the time or energy to be concerned about things that do not matter. They are not even in your awareness. With practice and conscious effort, you can maintain perspective and recognize when things do not matter when you are not dealing with a crisis. When you are able to do this, you will notice increased happiness.

Keeping things in perspective is a mindset that I often address in my therapy practice. I also speak about this in my online monthly membership community, Feeling Good with Dr. Peggy, where I teach methods of cultivating joy, resilience, gratitude, and meaning. Yes, it is important to do well on a project at work but making a mistake does not define you or bring down your worth. An argument with a friend does not mean the end of your social life. A difficult period with your teenager does not mean that you are a "bad" parent, or that the relationship will always be difficult.

Looking at the value behind what you are labeling as a problem can also help you to maintain perspective. For example, you may feel guilty missing dinner with your family because you value time with your family. You may feel disappointed in not achieving a goal because you value success. You may feel betrayed by a friend because you value trust. Look at the value to help you see the bigger, and more positive picture.

Take Action

1. What is bothering you right now? Ask yourself, "Does this really matter?" If you were experiencing a crisis now, would this still matter? Write the problem down. If this problem would not matter if you were in the midst of a crisis, release it. Rip up the piece of paper and throw it away; let it go.

2. If this problem does matter, what solutions do you have? If you do not have a solution to the problem, what can you do about your feelings? Use the same piece of paper where you wrote down the problem. If it does matter, write down what you can do about it. Then write down any small steps that you can take today toward addressing the

problem. If the problem is not in your control, allow yourself to process the related feelings. You can use techniques from the chapter, "Journal/Write About Thoughts and Feelings."

3. Look back on a time when you were going through a crisis. Did the "smaller" problems matter then? Remember this mindset and that you do not need to currently be experiencing a crisis in order to let go of fear.

4. When you think about the "big picture" and what really matters in your life, what positive experience, relationship, or situation do you have that you can celebrate? Take out a piece of paper or a journal and write down what really matters to you that you can celebrate. Not only will this help you gain perspective and feel better in the moment, but you can refer back to this list during times when you are bogged down by the smaller problems of life to help remind you what really matters to you.

Chapter 32

Focus on How Far You've Come, Not How Far You Have to Go

"Remember how far you've come, not just how far you have to go. You are not where you want to be, but neither are you where you used to be."
–Rick Warren

Whatever goal you are striving for, try not to get caught up in how far you have to go. Pay attention to thoughts such as, "I can't do this anymore," "I'll never get there," "I'm tired," "This is going to take too long," When it feels overwhelming, feels like it is taking too long and/or feels like too much effort, focus on how far you have come. Most of our goals take not just effort, but time, often a significant amount of time. If we only focused on how far we had to go, most of us would be discouraged, give up, and never reach the goal, leading to feelings of frustration, disappointment, and regret. Conversely, looking back on how far we have come can serve as a motivation, as an energizer, or an emotional boost to keep going and increases the chances of reaching a goal. This leads to happiness, fulfillment, and satisfaction.

Sometimes having a tangible measure of how far you have come can be helpful. Keep track, so that on the days that you feel like giving up, you can go back and revisit how far you've come. Keep a list of compliments, praise, and accomplishments. Keep track quantitatively by creating a numbered list and qualitatively by providing positive substance to the details.

If you are working on a goal that requires much time to achieve, you can also reward yourself at certain milestones. For example, if you are writing a book, you can reward yourself when you finish writing a chapter. If you are working on obtaining a degree, you can reward yourself with each completed class or semester.

Also, when we are reaching toward a goal and not quite there yet, frustration and disappointment can steal our joy in everyday living. Be mindful of enjoying your life exactly where you are today. Remember this quote: "You are exactly where you are supposed to be." Set your intention of the day to enjoy the moment and where you are on your journey toward achieving your goal, regardless of how far you have to go or how far you have come. Focus on the present moment. Find joy in the journey. This takes all judgment and evaluation out of the equation and instead allows you to simply focus and celebrate your life. I know that this can be very challenging when faced with financial, health, or other personal or professional struggles. There may be days when the joy is small and short-lived. Celebrate it anyway. While reaching your goal might be the ultimate reward, the path that got you there is also worthy of celebrating each step of the way.

Think about some high-profile people who have achieved success. They did not achieve their greatness overnight! We would be deprived of their contributions to the world if they kept focusing on how far they had to go, or got discouraged and quit at any point along the way. J.K. Rowling, author of the Harry Potter series, received dozens of rejections before landing a book deal for her 90,000-word manuscript. What if she gave up after 45,000 words? What if she gave up after the ninth rejection? It is hard to think of a world without Harry Potter!

Knowing the steps of your journey will help you achieve any long endeavor. I think of my knee surgeon. If he knew as a high school graduate that he wanted to become an orthopedic surgeon, he could have mapped out journey— four years of college, four years of medical school, and five years of residency—a goal that would take thirteen years! But if you know that in advance and focus on your progress and celebrate every milestone you achieve, you can maintain motivation, happiness, and fulfilment.

Take Action

1. Sit down and write out all that you have accomplished, big and small, personal and professional. Keep this somewhere so that you can refer to it when you are feeling down. Seeing all that you have accomplished in one place can help you realize that you really have accomplished a lot. This will help you feel better about where you are right now, as well as provide motivation in moving forward. Keep in mind that your progress need not be tangible. It can be a shift in mindset that's preparing you. It can be the knowledge that you have gained, or the relationships that you have cultivated.

2. For the difficult days, use mantras to stay focused on the present. Place these inspirational words on cards and place them wherever you frequent in order to provide a reminder to find joy in the present moment. Some are: "Find joy in the journey," "Life is a journey, not a destination," "You are exactly where you are supposed to be," and "Be patient. Trust in the process."

3. Purchase an inspirational gemstone bracelet for motivation. I designed an entire line of bracelets to help encourage and support you or someone you love. https://www.peggysmidnightcreations.com/line/inspiration/

Chapter 33

Be Still. Be Mindful

"Learning how to be still, to really be still and let life happen;
that stillness becomes a radiance."
–Morgan Freeman

Being mindful, or living in the present moment, is especially important in today's world of multitasking with constant activities on our ubiquitous electronics—stimulation of our senses from all directions. Mindfulness is intentionally paying attention to the present moment and being aware of one's thoughts and feelings without judgment. When we are mindful and living in the present moment, we increase happiness because we are not worrying about the future or feeling guilty or shameful about the past.

We have been hearing more about mindfulness in the past few years and for good reason. Mindfulness techniques induce the Relaxation Response, a state coined by Herb Benson, M.D.[136] The Relaxation Response is a state of reduced stress and has numerous physiological and emotional benefits. Being in this state of relaxation and reduced stress helps restore digestive functioning and bring blood pressure, heart rate, and hormones back to normal levels. With regular induction of the Relaxation Response, people report experiencing significantly less anxiety and a noticeable improvement in mood.

Although people have been practicing mindfulness for years, the mental and physical health benefits are becoming more well-known. Even brief interventions have been effective for reducing stress and anxiety.[137] Mindfulness techniques reduce unwanted feelings related to depression, anger, and frustration[138] and help relieve the symptoms of stress and anxiety that accompany chronic illness and problems in daily living for both patients and healthcare providers.[139] Mental health professionals are incorporating Mindfulness-Based Stress Reduction (MBSR), a program created by Jon Kabat-Zinn, Ph.D.,[140] and Mindfulness Based Cognitive Therapy (MBCT),[141] a program developed by Zindel Segal, Mark Williams, and John Teasdale based on Kabat-Zinn's MBSR, into their clinical practices. These mindfulness practices have been shown to lower blood pressure[142] and heart rate,[143] demonstrating achievement of that Relaxation Response introduced by Herbert Benson.

With advances in technology, studies in neuroscience demonstrate the positive impact that practicing mindfulness has on the brain. Specifically, an often reported benefit is an increase in attention due to changes in the anterior cingulate cortex.[144] Meditation has also been demonstrated to boost immune functioning by increasing antibodies to influenza.[145] In addition to addressing troubling emotions, mindfulness increases overall life satisfaction and fosters a sense of peace.[146] Here are some simple ways to incorporate mindfulness into everyday living:

Be still.

To balance and maintain a joyful nature, take a moment to simply be still. Sit in your favorite chair, turn off distractions, and close your eyes— but not with the intention to fall asleep. Listen to music and/or light a candle. Notice how you feel after even just five minutes of not moving or thinking.

Focus on your breath.

This practice is very simple and can be done anywhere. Sit in a recliner or propped up in bed. Place your hands folded on your stomach. Inhale and watch your abdomen and hands rise and fall with each breath (rather than your chest). Imagine filling a balloon in your stomach with the air. Focus on the breath and let any other thoughts drift away. If you struggle with thoughts, focus on repeating a word with each breath, such as "relax," "calm," or "peace."

Another breathing exercise I like is called "box breathing." It simply involved breathing into the count of four, holding the breath to the count of four, breathing out to the count of four, and pausing to the count of four, and repeat for as long as desired.

Breathing exercises help increase relaxation by activating the parasympathetic nervous system and lowering heart rate and blood pressure. They have been proven effective in helping people cope with troubling emotions, such as anxiety, anger, and depression.[147] Practice breathing exercises when you are calm, and you will be more likely to call upon this exercise when feeling frustrated or angry. The wonderful part about breathing exercises is that you can do it anywhere, and no one has to know what you are doing! I have worked with many professionals who were able to lower their perceived stress levels at work by incorporating breathing exercises into their workdays. For further reading on how one neurosurgeon incorporated breathing and meditation exercises into his work, read James Doty's *Into the Magic Shop*.

Use mindfulness apps.

Some popular ones are Mindfulness, Simple Habit, Headspace, Buddhas Brain, Breathe2Relax, Destressify Stress Relief, Calm, Zen Friend, Insight Timer, and Stop, Breath, and Think. You can download these apps onto your smartphone. Many provide you with the opportunity to choose the length of the mindfulness activity, music or no music, female voice, male voice, or no voice, and topic or issue (sleep, anxiety, eating). I have a friend who has to wait at a red traffic light for several minutes on her way to work. She makes use of the time by doing one of her two-minute mindfulness meditations during her daily commute.

Play.

You may believe that you are way too old to use playdough, draw with markers, or fill out a coloring book. However, these simple activities that have repetitive motion have a wonderful calming effect,[148] and encourage us to connect with our inner child. The simple act of kneading playdough or coloring with a marker induces a sense of relaxation. There is something special about connecting with our more childlike selves. Adult coloring books are becoming quite popular, and you can find them in your local pharmacy or bookstore.

Engage in a craft that involves repetition.

Crafters who knit, crochet, bead, or engage in anything that involves repeated motion are aware of the stress-reducing benefits of their craft. The repetitive nature of the movements helps achieve a meditative state of mind.

Engaging in a craft that requires repetitive movement is my favorite way to be still. Ten years ago, I took an adult class in making jewelry. I learned some basic techniques and materials to use. This was during a time when I used to write my forensic reports from 8:00 PM to midnight while my young children were sleeping. I had difficulty going straight to bed after writing about child abuse and neglect. So I would bead for a few minutes to unwind and be still. I soon found that I felt so much better going to sleep after I spent just a few minutes engaged in the repetitive motion of beading. Soon, I became addicted to this relaxing feeling, and I was making way more jewelry than I could ever possibly wear! So I decided to sell some items. For tax purposes, I had to create a company name, and the most appropriate was "Peggy's Midnight Creations." Now, you will find inspirational bracelets from my jewelry line in 20 stores around the country! It all started from my need to quiet my mind.

Use visual props.

Several kinds of visual props can increase mindfulness and induce relaxation. Take the Calm Glitter Jar. You can create your own.[149] Watching the glitter settle induces a soothing, calming effect. This is similar to watching snow fall in a snow globe or lava flow in a lava lamp. Or install an aquarium. Nature provides opportunities with leaves, snow, or falling rain. While watching, focus on your breathing.

Take Action

1. Gain awareness of when you feel frazzled. When are you not "present?" When are you busy doing so many different things that you lose awareness of what is around you and who is talking to you? Notice your behavior and bring yourself back to the present moment. Focus on who you are with. Pay attention to your senses, focusing on what you see, hear, and feel around you.

2. Keep it simple. The simpler, the better. You are more likely to follow through with a stillness or mindfulness activity when it is short and basic. Download the app Insight Timer, put a topic of interest in the search bar, such as "gratitude" or "self-compassion." Then choose your preferred length of time for the guided meditations provided. Or simply sit in a comfortable chair and do deep breathing for two to five minutes.

3. Make sure that your mindfulness practices are enjoyable. Some people prefer the simplicity of focused breathing. Other people like coloring. Discover what makes you happy.

4. Find the best time of day for you to incorporate just five minutes of stillness or mindfulness. This could be when you first get out of bed in the morning, on your way to work, at lunch, on your way home from work, or as part of your bedtime routine. When you do this on a regular basis, it's more likely to become habit and more likely to be effective when you need to use it during times of heightened anxiety to help induce calmness.

5. Pay attention to how you feel before and after you engage in a stillness or mindfulness activity. In addition, remember that there are physiological benefits (lowered blood pressure, lowered heart rate) that you may not even be aware of in the moment. If you have access to any methods of measurement, you could compare your results before and after a mindfulness exercise and see how you can control your own physiology! This biofeedback is particularly helpful during anxiety attacks or panic attacks. If you experience panic attacks, you may be interested in downloading the app PanicMechanic, developed by two psychologists at the University of Vermont. This app provides feedback regarding your body's response to fear, learning more about how your body responds to certain situations and triggers and providing you a sense of control. Watch a video describing how the app works here: http://panicmechanicapp.com/

6. The month of October 2018 was dedicated to mindfulness in the monthly membership, Feeling Good with Dr. Peggy. There you will find additional resources, videos, and downloadable worksheets related to mindfulness. https://drpeggydelong.thinkific.com/courses/feeling-good-with-dr-peggy

Chapter 34

Dare to Hope

"Once you choose hope, anything is possible."
–Christopher Reeve

When all else fails, hope. And there will be days when hope is all you have left. Hope for calm amidst chaos, hope for less emotional or physical pain, hope after lost love. I love the saying, "When the world says, 'Give up,' Hope whispers, 'Try one more time.'"

Having hope elevates mood, even if it is just a little bit, and even if it is just for a moment. You may not notice a change in mood, but having hope helps carry you through a difficult time. Hope helps you make choices that will lead to a more positive outcome. Hope makes getting out of bed less challenging when it feels like the world is crashing in on you.

How do I know this? Because I've been there. I have been in the dark place where it took every ounce of energy to get out of bed. I have been there where the day has been filled with unbearable fear and sorrow.

The day my fiancé Scott proposed to me in 1993, I had hope that we would have a long and happy marriage. Three months after he proposed and was told that he had cancer with a 15 percent chance of being alive in

12 months, I had hope that he would be in that 15 percent. When he was nearing death and the doctor said that he would not survive the weekend, I had hope that he would live another week. After he died, I had hope that I would one day feel less gut-wrenching, nauseating emotional pain. I had hope that I would one day find love again. And when I did have the courage to love again, I had hope that I would not experience loss. Hope is what carried me through during every stage.

Hope is important when you have a dream or a wish, and you want to make it reality. Without hope, how is it possible other than pure luck? Hope is even more important and powerful when you have a dream or idea that others shut down, think is crazy, or think is unattainable. In fact, I think hope is a necessary ingredient for achieving our goals. Hope makes it possible. How can anything be achieved without hope?

Think about it. How can you start a new business without hope that it will be successful, or at the very least, provide you with fulfillment? How can you begin a long endeavor, such as entering college, or graduate school, without hope that you will obtain your degree? How can you share a secret or intimate thought with a partner or best friend without hope that your secret will be kept? How can you apply for jobs after being let go from your company if you do not have hope that you will be hired?

There may be a dark time in your life when hope is all you have left. Then you need to hang on to hope with all you might. And do not for one second let anyone take it away from you. Even well-meaning people may try to take it away from you, thinking that it is in your best interest. As if stripping you of your hope will somehow protect you from disappointment.

I have an unfortunate experience with this as well. We were told that Scott would not survive the weekend, but he did. He not only survived, but he was getting better. We were celebrating that he was able to open his eyes and celebrating that he was able to speak. I suppose that the doctor was concerned that if we had hope and experienced joy that our pain upon his death would be even greater. I believe that he meant well, but he was so wrong. I will never forget his words. "I don't want you to have false hope," he said. "Scott might be doing well today, but it is not going to last." He repeated, "I don't want you to have false hope."

But what the doctor did not realize is that he made no sense. There is no such thing as "false" hope. There is only hope. Powerful, magical hope. On the days that hope is all you have left, hope is everything. There is nothing "false" about it.

If you speak to people about how they overcame hardship, most likely, hope will be mentioned. After losing a loved one, having hope that one day grief will be less intense is helpful. During the financial hardship of COVID-19, hope that their businesses would open and thrive helped business owners cope during a very difficult time. After surgery, hope of gaining physical strength helps people get through physical therapy. After natural disaster, hope that life can be rebuilt helps people get through dark days.

I am grateful that I have the valuable life lesson that hope is powerful, and that hope is everything. The beautiful thing about hardship is that it often comes with a gift of wisdom. A type of wisdom that can only be acquired through pain.

Take Action

1. Remember that hope makes things possible. Hope is a necessary ingredient, and sometimes the foundation of what beautiful things are to come.

2. Remember that there is no such thing as "false" hope. There is only hope.

3. Do not wait until you are in the middle of a crisis to hope. This may be where you need hope the most, and possibly where hope is all you have. But be proactive and don't let these situations be your first experiences with the power of hope.

The Final Way

Chapter 35

Ask for What You Want Out of Life

"Ask for what you want and be prepared to get it."
–Maya Angelou

When you practice my suggestions and recommendations in this book, you will develop and strengthen your own happiness and joy. It's a practice. You will be most successful when you understand that cultivating your own happiness is an ongoing process, that you deserve to be happy, and that no one can do it for you. You need to step up and ask for what you want out of your life. The following are concepts I've discussed throughout this book. I'm summarizing and highlighting them here to help you ask for what you want out of life. Asking is perhaps the most important and influential action you can take to receive what you want.

You are in control.

You need to understand that you are the master of your life. No one can make things happen like you can. Situations may happen that are beyond your control, but only you have the power to respond to them in a way that meets your goals and for what you want out of life. We create our own realities based on what we think, feel, and believe, and talk about. This is the foundation of The Law of Attraction.[150] Whatever you focus on, think about, read about, and talk about intensely, you're going to attract more of that into your life. What you want out of life is available to you, waiting for you to ask. But you have to take action to get it.

Be clear.

You are more likely to get what you want out of life when you are clear about your goals. Sometimes getting clear on what we want involves letting go of beliefs that hold us back. Beliefs such as, "Doing what I want is selfish," "Work needs to be hard and not enjoyable," "Money doesn't grow on trees." It is important to examine what beliefs are holding you back from getting what you want. It is not selfish to ask for what you want in life. Remember, you serve the world when you love doing what you do, and you do it with love, care, and grace.

Often when I am working with people on life satisfaction and happiness, they do not know what they want in life. I draw upon my own experiences and what helped me when I wanted a new direction in my private practice. Here are some exercises and activities that brought me clarity.

Make a list of what you LOVE to do.

Then think of ways you could actually make money doing it. Knowing exactly how you could make money is really not that important in the beginning. You will learn that you just need to know what you want, and you will be continually be shown the how. Once you are clear on the what and stay focused on it, the how will keep showing up. Your job is then to be open to the how through every person you meet and every opportunity that comes your way.

Meditate and ask for guidance.

If this is too difficult to do on your own, try some apps that simply focus on breathing or guided meditations. Some popular ones are Calm, Headspace, Insight Timer, Oak, Simple Habit, and Stop, Breathe, and Think. The idea is to help quiet the mind so that you can be more receptive to guidance and messages. Be open to every person you meet and look for opportunities. But most important, take action.

Be open to ideas while engaging in relaxing activities or in nature. This could be while hiking, walking, kayaking, or doing yoga. Also, don't dismiss the opportunity for ideas to come to you at mundane places either, such as the shower! This could happen at any place where you can get lost in your thoughts. Another exercise for guidance comes from Jack Canfield's *The Success Principles*. This exercise involves sitting down and visualizing and writing down your ideal life. This includes your financial life (income, house, car), your ideal career and job responsibilities, your free time, your ideal physical health, your ideal relationships with your family and friends, your personal life, and your ideal community. The clearer you are about these ideals, the better able you will be to achieve them because the decisions you make on a daily basis will be more in line with the life you desire.

The importance of asking.

Asking is so critical to achieving want you want out of life. You cannot do it alone. So ask the Universe. Ask your friends. Ask anyone! Pray or meditate. Just put it out there in ways that are comfortable for you. And be specific. The more specific you are, the easier you make it for the Universe, your friends, and others to respond. Let others know your dream. Ask for help. Ask, and dream big. When asking for what you want, it is important that the words be phrased in the positive. For example, "I want to be out of debt" is very different from "I am living a life of abundance."

It is also important to let others know about your dreams and ask them for help and support in achieving them. Friends want to help, but they can only help when they know your dreams! This goes for both your professional dreams and your personal dreams.

I would not be where I am today without asking. I finally decided that I had had enough of just thinking about turning my love for making jewelry into a business and just do it. The very first step involved asking.

With my first product in hand, The Gratitude Bracelet, I put on my big girl pants, my rockin' cowboy boots that I purchased while on a girls' trip to Aspen, a unique poncho crocheted by my mother, and some lipstick, and went in to four stores uninvited and unannounced and respectfully asked the store owner for a moment of her time. That request was granted, and I showed each of them The Gratitude Bracelet and asked if they would be interested in carrying it in their stores. They all said yes! But I had to ask! They did not even know I existed! I had to be responsible for taking that first step and ask.

At another point in my life, I went to a labyrinth at a convent near me. A friend of mine taught me to enter the labyrinth with a question and to ask for guidance. At the time, I was at a pivotal time with my private practice. I did not know whether to pursue what made the most money but took from my soul or take a risk and build my bracelet business, something that fuels my soul. In my bracelet business, I mainly work with gemstones because they have meaning. My favorite gemstone is rose quartz because it is the stone of love.

On a beautiful day of blue skies, I entered the brick labyrinth that is tucked behind the convent. I slowly entered, contemplating the question, "Do I pursue and market my forensic practice to pay the bills, or do I follow my heart and continue my passion for making jewelry?" I walked slowly, with one foot in the same linear path as the other. I was lost in my thoughts, and I suddenly found myself in the center of the labyrinth. I was disappointed, as I had not experienced any revelations or guidance with my question. I looked off into the distance at the bucolic rolling hills, and I took a deep breath. Then I looked down, and to my surprise, someone had placed two rose quartz nuggets right in the center of the labyrinth. I could not have possibly received a better answer to my question. Rose quartz, known as the stone of love, is my favorite gemstone to use when making inspirational bracelets.

The importance of believing.

After asking for what you want, it is also important that you believe that what you want it is within your reach. How can you possibly achieve it if you think that it is out of your reach? You unwittingly set up roadblocks to achieving your goals when you do not believe that you can achieve them. The difficulty with this is that many of our limiting beliefs are not even within our awareness. You can work on uncovering your limiting beliefs with the help of a therapist or use exercises in self-help books. I suggest doing some of the exercises in *Everything is Figureoutable* by Marie Forleo and *Innercise* by John Assaraff.

The importance of gratitude.

When striving toward goals and happiness, it is important to be thankful for what you have. This brings more of what you want into your life. Focus on what you have and do not focus on what you do not have. Keep your thoughts positive and grateful. You will never have enough if you are not grateful for what you already have.

The importance of visualization.

In asking for what you want out of life, being able to see that it's possible will help you to achieve it. As I point out in the chapter, "Use Your Imagination," visualizing your goal activates your reticular activating system (RAS). Imagine or visualize the details about your goal. What does it look like? What do you see? How will you feel? The more you can attach an emotion to what you are asking for, the more powerful the visualization becomes.

The importance of trust.

So often we know what we want, but we don't know how to get there. And not knowing how to get there scares us, or makes us uncomfortable, so we quit. If you know what you want, and you want it with deep passion, then the HOW will unfold. It is not possible to do this without trust.

In the book and the movie, *The Secret*, Jack Canfield described this in a way that really helped me. If you are driving at night from point A to point B, you cannot see how you will get there in the dark. But your headlights light up the way, showing you the way, so that you see all that you need to see in order to get to your destination. In order to get from point A to point B, it was not necessary to see the entire way ahead of you at once. It unfolded as needed. The same thing happens with a goal. But it has to involve a passion, and it has to involve trust.

Positive affirmations.

When seeking what you want out of life, positive affirmations are helpful.[151] When considering positive affirmations, it is important to keep some things in mind:

The affirmation in the present tense. Say, "I am" and not "I am going to" or "I will."

State the affirmation in the positive. Focus on what you want. Not what you do not want. For example, instead of, "I am living without physical pain," the affirmation would be, "I am living a life of health and wellness."

Be specific. What specific accomplishment or goal do you want to achieve? How much money do you want to earn?

Include feelings. How do you feel thinking that you have already achieved this goal? Grateful? Proud? Delighted? Happy? Our affirmations are more powerful when there is emotion attached to them.

Put your affirmations on 3x5 index cards. Review them three times a day, say them out loud, close your eyes and visualize them.

Take Action

1. It's important to believe. What beliefs do you have, possibly since childhood, that interfere with attaining your goals and dreams? It's important to address any limiting beliefs because they will keep coming up and interfere with achieving your goals if they are not addressed.

2. Focus on gratitude. What are you grateful for? This will help bring more of what you want into your life.

3. Remember that neuroscience demonstrates the power of visualization. It's important to visualize your goals. Don't get hung up on this being a mental image or picture. It can be an idea. Write down what you are asking for in your life. Include as many details as possible. Then sit in a comfortable position, close your eyes, and imagine or visualize these details, including what they feel like.

4. Have a plan for dealing rejection. You are likely to be rejected as you ask and work toward your dreams. Having a plan of action or positive mindset can soften the blow when this occurs. Remember that rejection is merely a perception. It only feels like rejection when you assign that meaning to it. One of my favorite mindset techniques to use in the face of perceived rejection is Jack Canfield's SWSWSWSW – Some Will, Some Won't, So What, Someone's Waiting.

5. Trust is important. Trust that when your why is strong, the how will unfold. Trust that opportunities will come your way. Also trust that when you continue to focus on and visualize your goals, you will recognize and take advantage of these opportunities. It will not happen all at once, and part of the trust involves taking one step at a time. Jack Canfield provides a helpful analogy in the movie and book *The Secret*. If you are driving your car from New York to California in the dark, you do not know how to get there, and you cannot see the way. But your headlamps provide just enough light on the roadway to

get you from one point to the next. This happens continuously until you've reached your destination to achieve your goal of arriving in California. When you need help maintaining trust, you can remember this analogy.

6. Practice positive affirmations every day related to asking for what you want out of life. Practice positive affirmations that you will achieve it. Write these affirmations down and place them around your home and car as reminders to practice them.

7. If you would like guidance or deeper work in any of these areas, I offer an 8-week, on-line course, The Law of Attraction in ACTION. This course helps you to take action on these important concepts, and action is crucial for progress, growth, and movement. For more information about all that is covered in the course, you can visit this website: https://drpeggydelong.thinkific.com/courses/the-law-of-attraction-in-action

Epilogue

The ideas from this book came from my childhood. They are simple ways of using our thoughts and behavior to live our best lives. They are particularly useful on difficult days. I applied them on challenging days during my childhood. Since they were effective in helping me feel better, I continued doing them into my adulthood. I put these strategies to the test during the most grueling time of my fiancé's diagnosis and treatment for cancer, his death, and my father's death shortly after. This remained an individual, private way that I tested these ways of coping.

Then COVID-19 hit, and for the first time in my life, the entire world in 2020 was dealing with a crisis at the same time. Once again, I had the opportunity to use these coping methods. Only this time, I was not the only one. This time, the entire world was affected.

Like so many others, the pandemic has been a time of loss, anxiety, and uncertainty for me. While I have not lost a loved one to the virus, this period has not been without hardship. I edited this book while my oldest was a senior in high school. She lost her prom, graduation, and opportunity to say good-bye to her classmates, teachers, and high school hallways. I'll be bringing her to college soon, and I will not be permitted to enter her dorm. In addition, I closed the physical doors of my private practice, an office that I have had for eighteen years, because I could not afford to pay rent for an empty office. Sadly, I have been unable to touch or get within six feet of my mother for five months in order to keep her safe and healthy.

Yet, I'm still happy. That is not to say that I do not experience sadness, anxiety, or grief. I do. I just don't get stuck there. As I've edited this book for the last time, I've used every single one of these coping methods to help me get through this difficult time. It's not just me. I have meaningful discussions with friends, family, and clients, and these strategies are working for them too. It has always been my mission to help people with approaches that work on difficult days. I am delighted to say that these techniques are now pandemic tested.

To help people around the world with living their best lives, and cope with the most difficult days, I formed a membership group as a companion to this book, "Feeling Good with Dr. Peggy: An On-line Community of Seekers of Gratitude, Joy, Resilience, and Meaning." If you're looking for additional support and a sense of community in your journey through life, you'll find it here in this group. More information is available at https://drpeggydelong.thinkific.com/courses/feeling-good-with-dr-peggy.

You are a powerful human being. You may not be able to control what goes on around you and outside of you, but you do have control over what goes on inside of you. You have the power to control your thoughts and behavior, which has great influence on your life and how you feel. You have the power to use your thoughts and behavior to live your best life. The simple methods covered in this book have worked for me throughout my life, have worked for friends and clients, and are backed by research. These practices work to make the most of your good days, and they are perhaps most effective on your difficult days. I cannot wait for you to realize how truly powerful you are.

FURTHER READING AND
Resources

Ch 1: Accept That "Life is Not Fair"
- Bernie Siegel, *Love, Medicine, and Miracles* (New York: Harper Perennial, 1998).
- Viktor E. Frankl, *Man's Search for Meaning* (Boston: Beacon Press, 2006).

Ch 2: Get Outside in Nature
- Qing Li, *Forest Bathing: How Trees Can Help You Find Health and Happiness* (New York: Viking, 2016).
- Wallace Nichols, *Blue Mind: The Surprising Science That Shows How Being Near, In, On, or Under Water Can Make You Happier, Healthier, More Connected, and Better at What You Do* (New York: Little, Brown, and Company, 2015).

Ch 5: Read
- Peggy Doherty DeLong, *I Can See Clearly Now: A Memoir about Love, Grief, and Gratitude* (Oracle, Arizona: Peacock Proud Press, 2019).

- Viktor Frankl, *Man's Search for Meaning* (Boston, MA: Beacon Press, 2006).

Ch 8: Connect with People
- Catherine Price, *How to Break Up with Your Phone* (New York: Ten Speed Press, 2018).

Ch 10: Surround Yourself with People Who Make You Feel Good
- Don Miguel Ruiz, *The Four Agreements* (San Rafael, CA: Amber-Allen Publishing, 2016).

Ch 11: Ask for Help and Accept Help
- Amanda Palmer, *The Art of Asking: How I Learned to Stop Worrying and Let People Help* (New York: Grand Central Publishing, 2015).
- Brené Brown *The Gifts of Imperfection* (Center City, Minnesota: Hazelden Publishing, 2010).
- Brené Brown, *Daring Greatly How the Courage to be Vulnerable Transforms the Way We Live, Love, Parent, and Lead* (New York: Avery, 2015)

Ch 14: Create and Nurture a Strong Social Support Network
- Melanie Katzman, *Connect First: 52 Simple Ways to Ignite Success, Meaning, and Joy at Work* (New York: McGraw-Hill Education, 2019).

Ch 15: Speak Your Truth
- Don Miguel Ruiz, *The Four Agreements* (San Rafael, CA: Amber-Allen Publishing, 2016).
- Brené Brown, *Daring Greatly: How the Courage to be Vulnerable Transforms the Way We Live, Love, Parent, and Lead* (New York: Avery, 2015).
- Jack Canfield, *The Success Principles: How to Get from Where You Are to Where You Want to Be* (New York: William Morrow Paperbacks, 2015).

Ch 18: Allow Yourself to Feel Unwanted and Painful Emotions

- Edith Eger, *The Choice: Embrace the Possible* (New York: Scribner, 2018).
- Edith Eger, *The Gift: Twelve Lessons to Save Your Life* (New York: Scribner, 2020).

Ch 19: Journal/Write About Thoughts and Feelings

- James Pennebaker and Joshua M. Smyth, *Opening Up by Writing it Down: How Expressive Writing Improves Health and Eases Emotional Pain* (New York: The Guilford Press, 2016).
- James Pennebaker and John Frank Evans, *Expressive Writing: Words that Heal by* (Enumclaw, WA: Idyll Arbor, 2014).

Ch 20: Don't Take Things Personally

- Don Miguel Ruiz, *The Four Agreements* (San Rafael, CA: Amber-Allen Publishing, 2016).

Ch 21: Forgive

- Brené Brown, *The Gifts of Imperfection* (Center City, Minnesota: Hazelden Publishing, 2010).
- Brené Brown, *Daring Greatly How the Courage to be Vulnerable Transforms the Way We Live, Love, Parent, and Lead* (New York: Avery, 2015).
- Katherine Schwarzenegger Pratt, *The Gift of Forgiveness* (New York: Pamela Dorman Books, 2020).
- Pastor Nadia Bolz-Weber in video – "Forgive Assholes" https://www.youtube.com/watch?v=VhmRkUtPra8

Ch 24: Change the Way You View the Things That Bother You

- 12 Common Types of Cognitive Distortions https://drpeggydelong.com/blog

Ch 25: Use Your Imagination

- Shakti Gawain, *Creative Visualization: Use the Power of Visualization to Create What You Want in Your Life* (Novato, California: New World Library, 2016).
- John Assaraf, *Innercise: The New Science to Unlock Your Brain's Hidden Power* (Cardiff, CA: Waterside Press, 2008).
- Website for John Assaraf: https://www.myneurogym.com/
- James Doty, *Into the Magic Shop* (New York: Avery, 2017).
- Shannon Irvine, The Epic Success Podcast

Ch 27: Be Goofy

- Brené Brown, *The Gifts of Imperfection: Let Go of You Who Think You're Supposed to Be and Embrace Who You Are* (Center City, Minnesota, Hazelden, 2010).

Ch 28: Develop a Gratitude Mindset

- John Kralik, *A Simple Act of Gratitude: How Learning to Say Thank You Changed My Life* (New York: Hatchette Books, 2011).

Ch 30: Practice Self-Care

- Emeran Mayer, *The Mind-Gut Connection: How the Hidden Conversation within our Bodies Impacts Our Mood, Our Choices, and Our Overall Health* (New York: Harper Wave, 2018).
- Cullen Hardy, *The Gut-Brain Connection: Altering Your Diet to Improve Your Emotional Health* (Amazon.com Kindle, 2014).
- Nicole Cain, *Gut Psychology: The Most Comprehensive and Empirically Researched Dietary Program for Mental Health* (Amazon.com Kindle, 2018).
- Gene Stone, *Forks Over Knives: The Plant-Based Way to Health* (New York: The Experiment, LLC, 2011).
- Alona Pulde and Matthew Lederman, *The Forks Over Knives Plan: How to Transition to the Life-Saving, Whole-Food, Plant-Based Diet* (New York: Atria Books, 2017).

- Evelyn Tribole and Elyse Resch, *Intuitive Eating: A Revolutionary Program that Works* (New York: Essentials, 2020)
- Glenn Livingston, *Never Binge Again: Reprogram Yourself to Think Like a Permanently Thin Person* (Windham, New Hampshire: Psy Tech Inc, 2015).
- Robert Rosenberg, *Sleep Soundly Every Night, Feel Fantastic Every Day: A Doctor's Guide to Solving Your Sleep Problems* (New York: Demos Health, 2014).

Ch 34: Be Still; Be Mindful

- James Doty, *Into the Magic Shop* (New York: Avery, 2017).
- Panic Mechanic app http://panicmechanicapp.com

Ch 35: Ask for What You Want Out of Life

- Jack Canfield, *The Success Principles: How to Get from Where You Are to Where You Want to Be* (New York: William Morrow Paperbacks, 2015).
- Ronda Byrne, *The Secret*, (New York: Atria Books, 2006).
- Marie Forleo, *Everything is Figureoutable*, (New York: Portfolio, 2019).

Acknowledgements

I would like to thank those who influenced the creation of this book.

Jeff Scotti of Scotti Designs developed my first professional website. When I first came to you for help, you suggested that I write a blog. This book is an expansion of that very first blog!

I am grateful to all the people who have asked me my whole life, "What do you do to be so happy?" You challenged me to really think about what I do. It's not a secret! Here it is, and I want to share it with you.

I feel fortunate for every therapy client who has trusted me for emotional healing and assistance with fostering joy.

Susana Fonticoba of Clear Path Marketing, thank you for connecting me with Laura Bush, PhD, and Peacock Proud Press.

My editor Wendy Ledger of VoType Editorial and Transcription Services provided thoughtful and meticulous editing, and ongoing support and encouragement. Jana Galvan, thank you for the gorgeous cover and interior layout. You designed and created what I dreamed of but could not articulate, moving me to tears when I first saw the result of your craft.

Throughout this process, Laura Bush of Peacock Proud Press advocated for my book. Thank you for encouraging me to find research to support each claim in my book, making it a much richer read. You are the definition of integrity.

My business mentor, Sarah Walton always held fast to a vision for me, even before I had it for myself.

And, finally, many thanks to every organization that has welcomed me to speak about happiness and mental health, including Nicole Smith and Room to Read, Women's Cornerstone and St. Luke Parish, Ralph Weaver and East West Connection Joy Connection, Sha Nacino and World Gratitude Summit, Marcella Gencarelli and Lakeland Bank, Dutchess Day School, Rosann Glommeau and LINC Socials, Lyle Smith and the Story Forge Podcast, Dorit Palvanov and the Confident, Energized, and Sexy Mama Podcast, Serwaa Anokye and the Fabulous and Fearless Lifestyle Guide Summit, Helen Archantou and YWCA of Northern New Jersey, Colleen Pine and The Inter-Faithfuls, Rutgers University Division of Continuing Studies, Believe, Inspire, Grow, Nicole Smith and Happy to Help Radio Show, Game On Girlfriend podcast with Sarah Walton, New City Library, Basking Ridge TogetHER, Kathryn Higgins and Perfect Harmony Yoga, Washington Township Public Library, Junie Moon and the Midlife Out Loud podcast, Nicoll Nadege and The Book House, Wake Up With Marci, Talking Live with Dr. Robi Ludwig, Ellen Eppie and Scooch A Mi Boutique, McCarter Theatre, Kaitlin Overton and No Dominion Theatre, Livingston Public Library, Jeriann Benton and 3 Chicks Boutique, Jessica Chapin and Imaginations Boutique, Women's Wellness New Jersey, Lady Boss Book Club, Story Slam of No Dominion Theatre, Arrowhead Lodge, Kim Hayward and Journey's Day Spa, Suzane Northrup Blog Talk Radio, Shelly Quintana and Bee You Yoga and Wellness, Hackettstown Public Library, Vicki Lynn Morgan and Teachable Moments in Business, Bernardsville Public Library, Garden State Social, Signs from the Other Side with Fern Ronay, Dave and

Geralyn and The Coffee Potter, Grief and Rebirth: Finding the Joy in Life Podcast with Irene Weinberg, Chester Public Library, Peapack Gladstone Bank Corporate Headquarters, New Jersey Psychologists for the Promotion of Child Welfare, Rutgers School of Social Work/New Jersey Department of Children and Families, Morris County West Holistic Moms Network, Liberty Corner Presbyterian Church, The Albrook School, The United Way, Kiddie Academy, Camp Sunshine, and St. James Roman Catholic Church.

ABOUT THE
Author

Dr. Peggy Doherty DeLong is a psychologist who was raised in bucolic Bernardsville, New Jersey. She runs a private practice in Long Valley, New Jersey where she specializes in assisting individuals and groups with fostering gratitude and cultivating joy in everyday living.

Dr. Peggy provides psychotherapy, teaches online courses, and facilitates a monthly membership group. Through her books and speaking engagements, she provides inspiration and guidance to those who want to live a joyful life. She is the owner of Peggy's Midnight Creations, where she designs inspirational, mental health bracelets for life's transitions and challenges.

An accomplished psychologist, entrepreneur, speaker, artist, and author, Dr. DeLong feels passionate about helping others live their very best lives, even on the worst of days. When she's not focused on her work, she loves spending time with her family in nature. Peggy enjoys downhill and telemark skiing, hiking, mountain biking, and watching sunsets from her kayak.

Would you like support on your journey?
Join Dr. Peggy's online membership community:
"Feeling Good with Dr. Peggy: Monthly Membership Community
for Seekers of Gratitude, Joy, Love, Resilience,
Fulfillment, and Meaning in Life"
https://drpeggydelong.thinkific.com/courses/feeling-good-with-dr-peggy

Visit her website:
https://drpeggydelong.com

Peggy loves to hear from her readers:
drpeggydelongpsych@gmail.com

Notes

1   Robert A. Emmons and Michael E. McCullough, "Counted Blessings Versus Burdens: An Experimental Investigation of Gratitude and Subjective Well-being in Daily Life," Journal of Personality and Psychology 84, (2003): 377-389.

2   Melissa Marselle, Katherine Irvine, and Sara Warber, "Examining Group Walks in Nature and Multiple Aspects of Well-Being: A Large-Scale Study," Ecopsychology 6, (2014): 134–147.

3   Richard J. Mitchell, Elizabeth A. Richardson, Niahmh K. Shortt, and Jamie R. Pearce, "Neighborhood Environments and Socioeconomic Inequalities in Mental Well-being," American Journal of Preventive Medicine 49, (2015): 80–88.

4   Jo Thompson Coon, Kate Boddy, Ken Stein, and Rebecca Whear, "Does Participating in Physical Activity in Outdoor Natural Environments Have a Greater Effect on Physical and Mental Wellbeing Than Physical Activity Indoors? A Systematic Review," Environmental Science and Technology 45, (2011): 1761–1772.

5   Gregory N. Bratman, Gretchen Daily, Benjamin Levy, and James Gross, "The Benefits of Nature Experience: Improved Affect and Cognition," Landscape and Urban Planning 138, (2015): 41–50.

6   Guy Winch, Emotional First Aid: Healing Rejection, Guilt, Failure, and Other Everyday Hurts (New York: Hudson Street Press, 2013).

7   Holli-Ann Passmore and Mark Holder, "Noticing Nature: Individual and Social Benefits of a Two-Week Intervention," Journal of Positive Psychology 12, no. 6 (2017): 537-546.

8   Midhiel van Elk, M. Andrea Arciniegas Gomez, Wietske Vander Zwaag, Hein T. Van Schie, and Disa Sauter, "The Neural Correlates of the Awe Experience: Reduced Default Mode Network Activity During Feelings of Awe," Human Brain Mapping 40, no. 12 (2019): 3561-3574.

9   Qing Li, Forest Bathing: How Trees Can Help You Find Health and Happiness (New York: Viking, 2018).

10 Wallace Nichols, Blue Mind: The Surprising Science That Shows How Being Near, In, On, or Under Water Can Make You Happier, Healthier, More Connected, and Better at What You Do (New York: Little, Brown, And Company, 2015).

11 Michael P. Kelley, Robert D. Coursey, and Peter M. Selby, "Therapeutic Adventures Outdoors: A Demonstration of Benefits for People with Mental Illness," Psychiatric Rehabilitation Journal 20, no. 4, (1997): 61-73.

12 Karmel W. Choi, Chia-Yen Chen, Murry B. Stein, et al., "Assessment of Bidirectional Relationships Between Physical Activity and Depression Among Adults: A 2-sample Mendelian Randomization Study," JAMA Psychiatry 74, no. 4, (2019): 399-408.

13 Mayo Clinic Staff, "Depression and Anxiety: Exercise Eases Symptoms," Mayo Clinic, 9/27/17, www.mayoclinic.org.

14 Babyak, M, Blumenthal J, Herman S et al. (2000). Exercise treatment of major depression: maintenance of therapeutic benefit at 10 months. Psychosomatic Medicine, 62 (5), 633-638).

15 Jasper A. Smitsand Michael W. Otto, Exercise for Mood and Anxiety: Proven Strategies for Overcoming Depression and Enhancing Well-being (New York: Oxford University Press, 2011).

16 Faith Ozbay, Douglas Johnson, Eleni Dimoulas et. al., "Social Support and Resilience to Stress: From Neurobiology to Clinical Practice," Psychiatry 4, no. 5 (2007): 35-40.

17 Melissa R. Marselle, Katherine N. Irvine, and Sara L. Warber, "Examining Group Walks in Nature and Multiple Aspects of Well-Being: A Large-Scale Study," Ecopsychology 6, no. 4 (2014): 134-147.

18 Michail Mantzios and Kyriaki Giannou, "When Did Coloring Books Become Mindful? Exploring the Effectiveness of a Novel Method of Mindfulness-Guided Instructions for Coloring Books to Increase Mindfulness and Decrease Anxiety," Frontiers in Psychology 9, (2018): 56.

[19] Dana Carsley and Nancy Heath, "Effectiveness of Mindfulness-Based Coloring for University Students' Test Anxiety," Journal of American College Health (2019):1-10.

[20] Cathy Malchiodi, The Soul's Palatte: Drawing on Art's Transformative Powers for Health and Wellbeing (Boston: Shambhala Publications, 2002).

[21] Catherine Kelly, Shirley Cudney, and Clarann Weinert, "Use of Creative Arts as a Complementary Therapy by Rural Women Coping with Chronic Illness," Journal of Holistic Nursing 30, no. 1 (2012): 48-54.

[22] Jill Riley, Betsan Corkhill, and Clare Morris, "The Benefits of Knitting for Personal and Social Wellbeing in Adulthood: Findings from an International Survey," British Journal of Occupational Therapy 76, no. 2 (2013): 50-57.

[23] Kelly Lambert, Lifting Depression: A Neuroscientist's Hands-On Approach to Activating Your Brain's Healing Power (New York: Basic Books, 2010).

[24] Sarah McKay, "Why Crafting Is Great For Your Brain: A Neuroscientist Explains," Mind Body Green, http://www.mindbodygreen.com/0-14252/why-crafting-is-great-for-your-brain-a-neuroscientist-explains.html

[25] Therese Rando, How to Go on Living When Someone You Love Dies (New York: Lexington Books, 1988).

[26] Betty Eadie, Embraced by the Light (Placerville, CA: Gold Leaf Press, 1994).

[27] David Lewis, "Galaxy Stress Research," Mindlab International, Sussex University (2009).

[28] Raymond A. Mar, Keith Oatley, and Jordan B. Peterson, "Exploring the Link Between Reading Fiction and Empathy: Ruling Out Individual Differences and Examining Outcomes," Communications 34, (2009): 407-428.

[29] Shira Gabriel and Ariana F. Young, "Becoming a Vampire without Being Bitten: The Narrative Collective-Assimilation Hypothesis," Psychological Science 22, (2001): 990-994.

[30] Raymond Mar and Keith Oatley, "The function of Fiction in the Abstraction and Simulation of Social Experience," Perspectives in Psychological Science 3, no. 3 (2008): 173-192.

[31] Vivian Howard, "The Importance of Pleasure Reading in the Lives of Young Teens: Self-Identification, Self-Construction, and Self-Awareness," Journal of Librarianship and Information Science 43 (2001): 46-55.

[32] H.J. Trapp, "Music and Health: What Kind of Music is Helpful for Whom? What Music Not?" Deutsche Medizinische Wochenschrift 134, no. 51-52 (2009): 2601-6.

[33] Valorie N. Salimpoor, Mitchel Benovoy, Kevin Larcher, Alain Dagher, and Robert J Zatorre, "Anatomically Distinct Dopamine Release During Anticipation and Experience of Peak Emotion to Music," Journal Nature Neuroscience 14, no. 2 (2011): 257-262.

[34] Thomas Schäfer, Peter Sedlmeier, Christine Städtler, and David Huron, "The Psychological Functions of Music Listening," Frontiers in Psychology 4 (2013): 511.

[35] Ann J. Blood and Robert J. Zatorre, "Intensely Pleasurable Responses to Music Correlate with Activity in Brain Regions Implicated in Reward and Emotion," Proceedings of the National Academy of Sciences 98, (2001): 11818–11823.

[36] Myriam V. Thoma, Roberto La Marca, Rebecca Brönnimann, Linda Finkel, Ulrike Ehlert, and Urs M. Nater, "The Effect of Music on the Human Stress Response," PLOSONE 8, no.8 (2013): e70156.

[37] Lyz Cooper, "Using Music as Medicine – Finding the Optimum Music Listening 'Dosage': An Excerpt of a Study," British Academy of Sound therapy (2013).

[38] Elli Polack, "New Cigna Study Reveals Loneliness Levels in America," Cigna.com, 5/1/2008, https://www.cigna.com/newsroom/news-releases/2018/pdf/new-cigna-study-reveals-loneliness-at-epidemic-levels-in-america.pdf

[39] Matthew Pittman and Brandon Reich, "Social Media and Loneliness: Why an Instagram Picture May be Worth More Than a Thousand Twitter words," Computers in Human Behavior 62 (2016): 155-167.

[40] Shimon Saphire-Bernstein and Shelley E. Taylor, "Close Relationships and Happiness," in Oxford Handbook of Happiness, ed. Ilona Boniwell, Susan A. David, and Amanda Conley Ayers (Oxford: Oxford University Press, 2013).

[41] Meliksah Demir, Metin Özdemir, ane Lesley Weitekamp, "Looking to Happy Tomorrows with Friends: Best and Close Friendships as They Predict Happiness," Journal of Happiness Studies 8 (2007): 243-271.

[42] Ryan Dwyer, Kostadin Kushlev, and Elizabeth Dunn, "Smartphone Use Undermines Enjoyment of Face-to-Face Social Interactions," Journal of Experimental Social Psychology 78, 2017.

[43] Kostadin Kushlev and Elizabeth Dunn, "Smartphones Distract Parents from Cultivating Feelings of Connection When Spending Time with Their Children," Journal of Social and Personal Relationships 36. No. 6, 2018.

[44] Susan Pinker, The Village Effect: How Face-to-face Contact Can Make Us Healthier and Happier (Toronto: Vintage Canada, 2015).

[45] N.J. Emerty, "The Eyes Have It: The Neuroethology, Function and Evolution of Social Gaze," Neuroscience and Biobehavioral Reviews 24, no. 6 (2000): 581-604.

[46] "Improving Your Child's Social Skills: Making Eye Contact," The Social Express, 3/4/2014, http://thesocialexpress.com/improving-childs-social-skills-making-eye-contact/

[47] Adrian F. Ward, Kristen Duke, Ayelet Gneezy, and Maarten W. Bos, "Brain Drain: The Mere Presence of One's Own Smartphone Reduces Available Cognitive Capacity," Journal of the Association for Consumer Research 2, no. 2 (April 2017): 140-154.

[48] Arnold Glass and Mengzue Kang, "Dividing Attention in the Classroom Reduces Exam Performance," Educational Psychology 39, no. 3 (2019): 395-408.

[49] Sherry Turkle, Reclaiming Conversation: The Power of Talk in the Digital Age (New York: Penguin Books, 2015).

[50] Frank J. Elgar, Wendy Craig, and Stephen J. Trites, "Family Dinners, Communication, and Mental Health in Canadian Adolescents," Journal of Adolescent Health 52, no. 4 (2013): 433–438.

[51] Mary Eisenberg, Rachel Olson, Diane Neumark-Sztainer, Mary Story, and Linda Bearinger, "Correlations Between Family Meals and Psychosocial Well-Being Among Adolescents," Archives of Pediatrics and Adolescent Medicine 158, no. 8 (2014): 792-796.

[52] "The Importance of Family Dinners VIII: A CASA Columbia White Paper" (paper presented at the National Center on Addiction and Substance Abuse at Columbia University, September, 2012), https://www.centeronaddiction.org/addiction-research/reports/importance-of-family-dinners-2012

[53] Peggy DeLong, "Ten Ideas to Make the Most of Family Dinners," Dr. Peggy DeLong, 12/11/2015, https://drpeggydelong.com/ten-ideas-to-make-the-most-of-family-dinners/

[54] Emily Blatchford, "Compliments are Good for Your Health, But Not if They're Fake," Huffington Post, 6/20/17, https://www.huffingtonpost.com.au/2017/06/19/compliments-are-good-for-your-health-but-not-if-theyre-fake

[55] Gerald Schoenewolf, "Emotional Contagion: Behavioral Induction in Individuals and Groups," Modern Psychoanalysis 15 (1990): 49–61.

[56] James H. Fowler and Nicholas Christakis, "Dynamic Spread of Happiness in a Large Scale Network: Longitudinal Analysis Over 20 Years in the Framingham Heart Study," British Medical Journal 337 (2008): a2338.

[57] Adam D. I. Kramer, Jamie E. Guillory, and Jeffrey T. Hancock, "Experimental Evidence of Massive-Scale Emotional Contagion Through Social Networks," Proceedings of the National Academy of Sciences 111, no. 24 (2014): 8778-8790.

[58] Y.K. Chan and Rance P.L. Lee, "Network Size, Social Support and Happiness in Later Life: A Comparative Study of Beijing and Hong Kong," Journal of Happiness Studies 7, no. 1 (2006): 87-112.

[59] https://www.njheartworks.org/

[60] Universitat Autònoma de Barcelona, "Resilient people more satisfied with life," ScienceDaily. (accessed August 15, 2019), www.sciencedaily.com/releases/2012/05/120523114726.htm

[61] Morley Glicken, "Helping Others as an Attribute of Resilience," in Learning from Resilient People: Lessons We Can Apply to Counseling and Psychotherapy (Thousand Oaks: SAGE Publications, 2006).

[62] Jorge Moll, Frank Krueger, Roland Zahn, Matteo Pardini, Ricardo de Oliveira-Souza, and Jordan Grafman, "Human Fronto–Mesolimbic Networks Guide Decisions About Charitable Donation," Proceedings of the National Academy of Sciences, 2006.

[63] Rachel Piferi and Kathleen Lawler, "Social Support and Ambulatory Blood Pressure: An examination of Both Giving and Receiving," International Journal of Psychophysiology 62, no. 2 (2006): 328-336.

[64] Keito Otake, Satoshi Shimai, Junko Tanaka-Matsumi, Kanako Otsui, and Barbara Frederickson, "Happy People Become Happier Through Kindness: A Counting Kindness Intervention," Journal of Happiness Studies 7, no. 3 (2006): 361-375.

[65] Y. Joel Wong, Jesse Owen, Nicole T. Gabana, Joshua W. Brown, Sydney McInnis, Paul Toth, and Lynn Gilman, "Does Gratitude Writing Improve the Mental Health of Psychotherapy Clients? Evidence from a Randomized Controlled Trial," Psychotherapy Research 28, no. 2 (2018): 192-202.

[66] Francesca Borgonovi, "Doing Well by Doing Good: The Relationship Between Formal Volunteering and Self-Reported Health and Happiness," Social Science and Medicine 66 (2008): 2321-2334.

[67] Eric S. Kim, Ashley V. Whillans, Matthew T. Lee, Ying Chen, and Tyler J. VanderWeele, "Volunteering and Subsequent Health and Well-Being in Older Adults: An Outcome-Wide Longitudinal Approach," American Journal of Preventive Medicine, (2020): 1-11.

[68] Elizabeth Dunn and Lara Aknin, "Spending Money on Others Promotes Happiness," Science 319 (2018): 1687.

[69] Shawn Achor, The Happiness Advantage (New York: Crown Publishers, 2010).

[70] Elli Polack, "New Cigna Study Reveals Loneliness Levels in America," Cigna.com, 5/1/2008, https://www.cigna.com/newsroom/news-releases/2018/pdf/new-cigna-study-reveals-loneliness-at-epidemic-levels-in-america.pdf.

[71] Faith Ozbay, Douglas Johnson, Eleni Dimoulas et al, "Social Support and Resilience to Stress: From Neurobiology to Clinical Practice," Psychiatry 4, no. 5 (2007): 35-40.

[72] Marilyn Hockenberry-Eaton,Virginia Kemp, and Colleen DiIorio, "Cancer Stressors and Protective Factors: Predictors of Stress Experienced During Treatment for Childhood Cancer," Research in Nursing and Health 17, (1994): 351-361.

[73] Sheldon Cohen, Thomas Ashby Wills, "Stress, Social Support and the Buffering Hypothesis," Psychological Bulletin, 98 (1988): 310-357.

[74] N.J. Emerty, "The Eyes Have It: The Neuroethology, Function and Evolution of Social Gaze," Neuroscience and Biobehavioral Reviews 24, no. 6 (2000): 581-604.

[75] "Prime Minister Theresa May Launches Government's First Loneliness Strategy," Gov.UK, last modified October 16, 2018, https://www.gov.uk/government/news/pm-launches-governments-first-loneliness-strategy.

[76] "COVID Response Tracking Study," NORC at University of Chicago, June, 2020, https://www.norc.org/Research/Projects/Pages/covid-response-tracking-study.aspx

[77] Sheldon Cohen, Thomas Ashby Wills, "Stress, Social Support and the Buffering Hypothesis," Psychological Bulletin, 98 (1988): 310-357.

[78] Martin Seligman and Mihaly Csikszentmihalyi, "Positive Psychology: An Introduction," American Psychologist 55, no. 1 (2000): 5-14.

[79] Fariba Pourjali and Maryam Zharnaghash. Relationships Between Assertiveness and the Power of Saying No with Mental Health Among College Students," Procedia Social and Behavioral Sciences 9 (2010): 137-141.

[80] Leon Festinger, "A theory of social comparison processes," Human Relations 7, no. 2 (1954): 117-140.

[81] Phillip Ozimek and Hans-Werner Bierhoff, "All My Online-Friends are Better Than Me – Three Studies About Ability-Based Comparative Social Media Use, Self-Esteem, and Depressive Tendencies," Behaviour and Information Technology, 2019.

[82] Steven C. Hayes, Kirk D. Strosahl, and Kelly G. Wilson, Acceptance and Commitment Therapy, Second Edition: The Process and Practice of Mindful Change (New York: Guilford Press, 2012).

[83] Marlene Bullock, "Reiki: A Complementary Therapy for Life," American Journal of Hospice and Palliative Medicine 14, no. 1 (1997): 31-33.

[84] Katherine M. Krpan, Ethan Kross, Marc Berman, Patricia Deldin, Mary Askren, and John Junides, "An Everyday activity as a treatment for depression: The Benefits of Expressive Writing for People Diagnosed with Major Depressive Disorder," Journal of Affective Disorders 150 (2013): 1148-1151.

[85] Philip Ulrich and Susan Lutgendorf, "Journaling About Stressful Events: Effects of Cognitive Processing an Emotional Expression," Annals of Behavioral Medicine 24 (2002): 244-250.

[86] Karen A. Baike and Kay Wilhelm, "Emotional and Physical Health Benefits of Expressive Writing," Advances in Psychiatric Treatment 11 (2005): 338-346.

[87] Sigmund Freud, "Three essays on the Theory of Sexuality," American Journal of Psychiatry 148, no. 12 (1905): 1733-1735.

[88] Jerry L. Deffenbacher, David M. Deffenbacher, Rebekah S. Lynch, and Tracy L. Richards, "Anger, Aggression and Risky Behavior: A Comparison of High and Low Anger Drivers," Behaviour Research and Therapy 41, no. 6 (2003): 701-718.

[89] Tara E. Galovski. Edward B. Blanchard, "The Effectiveness of a Brief Psychological Intervention on Court-Referred and Self-Referred Aggressive Drivers," Behaviour Research and Therapy 40, no. 12 (2002): 1385-1403.

[90] Linda Cox Broyles, "Resilience: Its Relationship to Forgiveness in Older Adults," (PhD thesis, University of Tennessee, 2005), https://trace.tennessee.edu/cgi/viewcontent.cgi?article=3294andcontext=utk_graddiss.

[91] Michael A. Cohn, Barbara L. Fredrickson, Stephanie L. Brown, Joseph A. Mikels, Anne M. Conway, "Happiness Unpacked: Positive Emotions Increase Life Satisfaction by Building Resilience," Emotion 9, no. 3 (2009): 361–368.

[92] Larry Cahill and James McGaugh, "A Novel Demonstration of Enhanced Memory Associated with Emotional Arousal," Consciousness and Cognition 4, no. 4 (1995): 410-421.

[93] Meaghan A. Barlow, Carsten Wrosch, Jean-Philippe Gouin, Ute Kunzmann, "Is Anger, but Not Sadness, Associated With Chronic Inflammation and Illness in Older Adulthood?" Psychology and Aging 34, no. 3 (2019): 330 –340.

[94] Xiaobo Yu and Guanhua Fan, "Direct and Indirect Relationship Between Locus of Control and Depression," Journal of Health Psychology 21, no. 7 (2016).

[95] Suzanne Segerstrom, Jennie C.I. Tsao, Lynn E. Alden, and Michelle G. Craske, "Worry and Rumination: Repetitive Thought as a Concomitant and Predictor of Negative Mood," Cognitive Therapy and Research 24, no. 6 (2000): 671-688.

[96] Christina Hibbert, "How Do I Grieve?": Grief Work and Tears," Dr. Christina Hibbert, https://www.drchristinahibbert.com/dealing-with-grief/how-do-we-grieve-grief-work-and-tears/

[97] William H. Frey, Crying: The Mystery of Tears (Washington: D.C., Winston Press, 1985).

[98] Leonie Kronborg, Margaret Plunkett, Nicholas Gamble, and Yvette Kaman, "Control and Resilience: The Importance of an Internal Focus to Maintain Resilience in Academically Able Students," Gifted and Talented International 32, no.1 (2017): 59-74.

[99] Xiaobo Yu and Guanhua Fan, "Direct and Indirect Relationship Between Locus of Control and Depression," Journal of Health Psychology 21, no. 7 (2016): 1293-1298.

[100] Aaron T. Beck, Gary Emery, and Ruth L. Greenberg, Anxiety disorders and phobias: A cognitive perspective (New York, Basic Books, 2005).

[101] John Assaraf, Innercise: The New Science to Unlock Your Brain's Hidden Power (Cardiff, CA: Waterside Press, 2008).

[102] Bettina S. Wiese, "Successful Pursuit of Personal Goals and Subjective Well-Being," in Personal Project Pursuit: Goals, Action and Human Flourishing, eds. Brian Little, Katariina Salmela-Aro, and Susan D. Phillips (Hillsdale, NJ: Lawrence Erlbaum, 2007), 301-328.

[103] Laura A. King, "The Health Benefits of Writing about Life Goals," Personality and Social Psychology Bulletin 27, (2001): 798-807.

[104] Svetla Velikova, Haldor Sjaaheim, and Bentw Nordtug, "Can the psycho-Emotional State Be Optimized by Regular Use of Positive Imagery? Psychological and Electroencephalographic Study of Self-Guided Training," Frontiers in Human Neuroscience 10 (2017).

[105] Nader N. Youssef, Joel R. Rosh, Mary Loughran, Stephanie G. Schuckalo, Ann N. Cotter, Barbara G. Verga, and Richard L. Mones, "Treatment of Functional Abdominal Pain in Childhood With Cognitive Behavioral Strategies," Journal of Pediatric Gastroenterology and Nutrition 39, no. 2 (2004): 192-196.

[106] Peter R.Giacobbi, Meagan E.Stabler, Jonathan Stewart, Anna-Marie Jaeschke, Jean L.Siebert, and George A. Kelley, "Guided Imagery for Arthritis and Other Rheumatic Diseases: A Systematic Review of Randomized Controlled Trials," Pain Management Nursing 16, no. 5 (2015): 792-803.

[107] Michael Von Korff and Gregory Simon, "The Relationship Between Pain and Depression," The British Journal of Psychiatry 168, no. S30 (1996), 101-108.

[108] Martin Seligman, Flourish: A Visionary New Understanding of Happiness and Well-Being (New York: Free Press, 2011).

[109] Sheldon Cohen and Thomas A. Wills, "Stress, Social Support and the Buffering Hypothesis," Psychological Bulletin 98 (1988): 310-357.

[110] Adrienne Wood, Magdalena Rychlowska, Sebastian Korb, and Paula Niedenthal, "Fashioning the Face: Sensorimotor Stimulation Contributes to facial expression recognition," Trends in Cognitive Sciences 20, no. 3 (2016): 227-240.

[111] Richard D. Lane, "Neural Correlates of Conscious Emotional Experience," In Richard D. Lane and Lynn Nadel (Eds.), Series in Affective Science: Cognitive Neuroscience of Emotion (New York, Oxford University Press, 2000): 345-370.

[112] Brian Luke Seaward, Managing Stress: Principles and Strategies for Health and Well-Being (Sudbury, MA, Jones and Bartlett, 2009).

[113] Robert Soussignan, "Douchenne Smile, Emotional Experience, and Autonomic Reactivity: A Test of the Facial Feedback Hypothesis," Emotion 2, no. 1 (2002): 52-74.

[114] Krystyna S. Aune and Norman C. H. Wong, "Antecedents and Consequences of Adult Play in Romantic Relationships," Personal Relationships: Journal of the International Association for Relationship Research 9, no. 3 (2002): 279-286.

[115] Leslie A. Baxter, "Forms and Functions of Intimate Play in Personal Relationships," Human Communication Research 18, no. 3, (1992): 336–363.

[116] Antonio Damasio and Gil Carvalho, "The Nature of Feelings: Evolutionary and Neurobiological Origins," Nature Reviews Neuroscience 14 (2013): 143-152.

[117] Tal Shafir, "Using Movement to Regulate Emotion: Neurophysiological Findings and Their Application to Psychotherapy," Frontiers in Psychology 7 (2016): 1451.

[118] Tal Shafir, Stephan Taylor, Anthony Atkinson, Scott Langenecker, and Jon-Kar Zubieta, "Emotion Regulation Through Execution, Observation, and Imagery of Emotional Movements," Brain and Cognition 82, no. 2 (2013): 219-277.

[119] Anna Bruk, Sabine Scholl, and Herbert Bless, "Beautiful Mess Effect: Self–Other Differences in Evaluation of Showing Vulnerability," Journal of Personality and Social Psychology 115, no. 2 (2018): 192-205.

[120] Alex M. Wood, Stephen Joseph and John Maltby, "Gratitude Uniquely Predicts Satisfaction with Life: Incremental Validity Above the Domains and Facets of the Five Factor Model," Personality and Individual Differences 45, no. 1 (2008): 49-54.

[121] Alex M.Wood, John Maltby, Raphael Gillett, P. Alex Linley, and Stephen Joseph, "The Role of Gratitude in the Development of Social Support, Stress, and Depression: Two Longitudinal Studies," Journal of Research in Personality 42, no. 4 (2008): 854-871.

[122] Alex M.Wood, Stephen Joseph, Joann Lloyd, and Samuel Atkins, "Gratitude Influences Sleep Through the Mechanism of Pre-Sleep Cognitions," Journal of Psychosomatic Research 66, no. 1 (2009): 43-48.

[123] Michael E. McCullough, Robert Emmons, and Jo-Ann Tsang, "The Grateful Disposition: A conceptual and Empirical Topography," Journal of Personality and Social Psychology 82, no. 1, (2002): 112-127.

[124] Michael E. McCullough and Robert A. Emmons, "Counting Blessings Versus Burdens: An Experimental Investigation of Gratitude and Subjective Well-Being in Daily Life," Journal of Personality and Social Psychology 84, no. 2 (2003): 377–389.

[125] Barbara L. Fredrickson, Marcial F. Losada, "Positive Affect and the Complex Dynamics of Human Flourishing," American Psychologist 60, no. 7 (2005): 678-686.

[126] Bernard J. Jaworski, Ajay K. Kohli, "Supervisory Feedback: Alternative Types and Their Impact on Salespeople's Performance and Satisfaction," Journal Of Marketing Research 28, no. 2 (1991): 190-201.

[127] "31 Benefits of Gratitude: The Ultimate Science-Backed Guide," Happier Human, last updated February 27, 2020, http://happierhuman.com/benefits-of-gratitude/.

[128] Barbara Frederickson, "The Value of Positive Emotions: The Emerging Science of Positive Psychology is Coming to Understand Why It's Good to Feel Good," American Scientist 91, (2003): 330-335.

[129] Shawn Achor, The Happiness Advantage (New York: Crown Publishers, 2010).

[130] Y. Joel Wong, Jesse Owen, Nicole T. Gabana, Joshua W. Brown, Sydney McInnis, Paul Toth, and Lynn Gilman, "Does Gratitude Writing Improve the Mental Health of Psychotherapy Clients? Evidence from a Randomized Controlled Trial", Psychotherapy Research 28, no. 2 (2018): 192-202.

[131] Nathaniel M. Lambert, Margaret S. Clark, Jared Durtshi, Frank D. Fincham, and Steven Graham, "Benefits of Expressing Gratitude: Expressing Gratitude to a Partner Changes One's View of the Relationship," Psychological Science, 21, no. 4(2010): 574-580.

[132] Els van der Helm and Matthew P. Walker, "Overnight Therapy? The Role of Sleep in Emotional Brain Processing," Psychological Bulletin 135, no. 5 (2009): 731–748.

[133] Fahimeh Haghighatdoost, Awat Feizi, Ahmad Esmaillzadeh, Nafiseh Rashidi-Pourfard, Ammar Hassanzadeh Keshteli, Hamid Roohafza, and Payman Adibi, "Drinking Plain Water is Associated with Decreased Risk of Depression and Anxiety in Adults: Results from a Large Cross-Sectional Study," World Journal of Psychiatry 8, no. 3 (2018): 88-96.

[134] Barbara Fredrickson, Positivity: Groundbreaking Research Reveals How to Embrace the Hidden Strength of Positive Emotions, Overcome Negativity, and Thrive (New York: Crown Publishers/ Random House, 2009).

[135] Jennifer A. Harrington and Virginia Blankenship, "Ruminative Thoughts and Their Relation to Depression and Anxiety," Journal of Applied Social Psychology 32, no. 3, (2006): 465-485.

[136] Herbert Benson and Miriam Klipper (1975). The Relaxation Response (New York: HarperCollins Publishers, 1975).

[137] David Call, Lynsey Miron, and Holly Orcutt," "Effectiveness of Brief Mindfulness Techniques in Reducing Symptoms of Anxiety and Stress," Mindfulness 5, no. 6 (2014): 658–668.

[138] Aishwarya Raj, and Pradeep Kumar, "Efficacy of Mindfulness Based Stress Reduction(MBSR): A Brief Overview," Journal of Disability Management and Rehabilitation 4, no. 1 (2018): 73-81.

[139] Sharon Praissman, "Mindfulness-based Stress Reduction: A Literature Review and Clinician's Guide," Journal of the American Academy of Nurse Practitioners 20 (2008): 212–216.

[140] Jon Kabat-Zinn, "Mindfulness-Based Stress Reduction," Constructivism in the human Sciences 8, no. 2 (2003): 73-107.

[141] Zindel V. Segal, J. Mark G. Williams, and John D. Teasdale, Mindfulness-Based Cognitive Therapy for Depression (New York: The Guilford Press, 2003).

[142] Paola Helena Ponte Márquez, Albert Feliu-Soler, María José Solé-Villa, Laia Matas-Pericas, David Filella-Agullo, Montserrat Ruiz-Herrerias, Joaquím Soler-Ribaudi, Alex Roca-Cusachs Coll, and Juan Antonio Arroyo-Díaz, "Benefits of Mindfulness Meditation in Reducing Blood Pressure and Stress in Patients with Arterial Hypertension," Journal of Human Hypertension, 33 (2019): 237–247.

[143] Annette M. Mankus, Amelia Aldao, Caroline Kerns, Elena Wright Mayville, and Douglas S. Mennin, "Mindfulness and Heart Rate Variability in Individuals with High and Low Generalized Anxiety Symptoms," Behaviour Research and Therapy 51 (2013): 386-391.

[144] Yi-Yuan Tang, Britta K. Hölzel, and Michael I. Posner, "The Neuroscience of Mindfulness Meditation," Nature Reviews Neuroscience 16, (2015): 213–225.

[145] Richard J. Davidson, Jon Kabat-Zinn, Jessica Schumacher, Melissa Rosenkranz, Daniel Muller, Saki F. Santorelli, Ferris Urbanowski, Anne Harrington, Katherine Bonus, John F. Sheridan, "Alterations in Brain and Immune Function Produced by Mindfulness Meditation," Psychosomatic Medicine 66, no. 1 (2004): 149-152.

[146] Matthew A. Killingsworth, Daniel T. Gilbert, "A Wandering Mind Is an Unhappy Mind," Science 330, no. 6006 (2010): 932.

[147] Xiao Ma, Zi-Qi Yue, Zhu-Qing Gong, Hong Zhang, Nai-Yue Duan, Yu-Tong Shi, Gao-Xia Wei, and You-Fa Li, "The Effect of Diaphragmatic Breathing on Attention, Negative Affect and Stress in Healthy Adults," Frontiers in Psychology 8 (2017): 874.

[148] Jayde A. M Flett, Celia Lie, Benjamin C. Riordan, Laura M. Thompson, Tamlin S. Conner, and Harlene Hayne, "Sharpen Your Pencils: Preliminary Evidence that Adult Coloring Reduces Depressive Symptoms and Anxiety," Creativity Research Journal 29, no. 4 (2017): 409-416.

[149] Lauren Stockly, "Calm Bottle (AKA Glitter Jar, AKA Mind Jar)," Creative Play Therapist, July 28, 2019, http://creativeplaytherapist.com/calm-bottle-aka-glitter-jar-aka-mind-jar/

[150] Rhonda Byrne, The Secret (New York: Atria Books, 2006).

[151] Geoffrey L. Cohen, David Keith Sherman, "The Psychology of Change: Self-Affirmation and Social Psychological Intervention," Annual Review of Psychology 65 (2014): 333-371.

Made in the USA
Middletown, DE
19 August 2023